A HISTORICAL TOUR

OF THE HOLY LAND

BERYL RATZER

gefen
publishing house בית הוצאה לאור
JERUSALEM ◆ NEW YORK   Est. 1981

Cover design: S. Kim Glassman
Photography: Hanan Isachar, Chanan Gertraide, Ami Wallach, Yuri Costa, Yoel Amster Ltd., Beryl Ratzer
Maps: N. Vitkon
Design: Angala Watson
Second print by: Etty Boochny, Nitzan Mandelbaum, N.M.I. Enterprises

The Scripture quotations contained herein are from *The Holy Scriptures: A Jewish Bible According to the Masoretic Text* (Tel Aviv: Sinai Publishing, 1966), and are used by permission. All rights reserved. Verse numbering occasionally deffers from that in other translations.

Photo on page 108 used by permission of Todd Bolen, BiblePlaces.com.
Photo on pages 87, 155 from Wikipedia.
Photo on page 144 courtesy of David Rubinger, Israel National Photo Collection (GPO)

Edition 9   8   7   6   5   4   3   2   1

Revised and Enlarged Edition 2010

Gefen Publishing House
6 Hatzvi Street
Jerusalem 94386, Israel
972-2-538-0247
orders@gefenpublishing.com

Gefen Books
600 Broadway
Lynbrook, NY 11563, USA
1-800-477-5257
orders@gefenpublishing.com

www.gefenpublishing.com

Printed in Israel

Send *for our free catalogue*

Library of Congress Cataloging-in-Publication Data
Ratzer, Beryl, 1939-....
A Historical Tour of the Holy Land: A Concise History of the Land of Israel with Photographs and Illustrations – Revised and enlarged edition.

ISBN 978-965-229-492-0
1. Palestine – History.   2. Israel – History.   3. Palestine – Antiquities.   I. Title.
DS118.R35 1999
956.94—dc21

99-043809
CIP

TO THE READER

The inspiration for *A Historical Tour of the Holy Land* and its planned companion, *A Historical Tour of the Bible*, came from the many questions asked by the people I have guided over the years. Thank you all.

This volume is not only for those who have visited Israel and want a souvenir that is more than a collection of beautiful photographs. It is also for those interested in, or intrigued by, the long and often turbulent history of the Holy Land.

As the Bible, both the Hebrew and Christian scriptures, has been used only as a source for historical knowledge, this book is equally suitable for readers of all religions or no religion at all.

History, for me, used to be about forgotten events and dead people. Through archaeological excavations, history has come alive. I can sense the people and events that passed through this piece of land, wedged between Egypt and the Fertile Crescent. Perhaps this book can convey that feeling to you, the reader.

The length of the chapters differs due to the varied amount of written sources for each period and to the fact that, while sometimes this area was a major player on the stage of history, at others it was desolate and unimportant — not even a minor role!

The speed at which the first two editions sold surprised even my optimistic family! This, the third edition, has been updated to the events of 2009.

If your appetite is whetted for more, the bibliography is a good place to begin. A visit is even better.

B.R.

My thanks to those who inspired me to write
and to those who converted my computer pages into a real book;
to my readers who made this third edition possible;
to my family,
who kept me going when
I felt that I had bitten off more than I could chew;
and finally, to my husband,
who, in addition to everything else, also carried my cameras.

CONTENTS

CHRONOLOGY OF HISTORICAL PERIODS

Sometimes different names have been used for identical or overlapping periods, depending on the historical events they encompass. The following table highlights those parallel periods and their time frames. The dates are those which are generally accepted, but you may well have a reference book with slightly different dates.

4000 - 3150 BCE   **Chalcolithic Age**

3150 - 1200 BCE   **Early, Middle and Late Bronze Ages**

1200 - 586 BCE   **Iron Age, Israelite Period**

          c. 955 - 586 BCE   First Temple

          c. 1030 - 928 BCE   United Kingdom

          c. 928 - 586 BCE   Kingdom of Judah

          c. 928 - 723 BCE   Kingdom of Israel

---

538 - 333 BCE   **Persian Period**

          515 BCE - 70 CE   Second Temple

---

333 - 63 BCE   **Hellenistic Period**

          166 - 37 BCE   Hasmonean Dynasty

---

63 BCE - 633 CE	**Roman Period**	
	63 BCE - 333 CE	Roman Pagan
	70 - c. 450	Mishnah and Talmud
	333 - 633	Byzantine Period

633 - 1099	**Arab Period**

1099 - 1291	**Crusader Period**

1291 - 1517	**Mameluke Period**

1517 - 1917	**Ottoman Period**

1917 - 1948	**British Mandate**	
	1920 - 1948	League of Nations

1948 -	**State of Israel**

c.: circa (approximate date)

BCE (before common era) and CE are the alternative designations for BC and AD in academic publications

DISTANCES (as the crow flies)

Metullah to Eilat	550 km/350 miles
Acco to Jordan River	50 km/31 miles
Netanya to 1949 Armistice Line	16 km/10 miles
Tel Aviv to Jordan River	70 km/44 miles
Ashdod to Jerusalem	57 km/36 miles
Kinneret (Sea of Galilee)	212 meters/650 feet below sea level, max. length & width: 20 km x 12 km / 12 miles x 7.5 miles
Dead Sea	400 meters/1300 feet below sea level, max. length & width: 75 km x 17 km / 47 miles x 11 miles

PLACES ON MAP - NUMERICALLY

1. Metullah Z-A
2. Banias Z-A
3. Dan Z-A
4. Kiryat Shmona Z-A
5. Hatzor Z-A
6. Safed Z-B
7. Katzrin Z-B
8. Rosh HaNikra Y-A
9. Acco Y-B
10. Haifa X-B
11. Beit Shearim Y-B
12. Sepphoris/Zippori Y-B
13. Horns of Hittin Y-B
14. Capernaum Z-B
15. Tiberias Z-B
16. Nazareth Y-B
17. Atlit X-C
18. Jezre'el Y-C

19. Megiddo Y-C
20. Beit Shean Z-C
21. Zichron Ya'acov X-C
22. Caesarea X-C
23. Netanya X-D
24. Nablus/Shechem Y-D
25. Shiloh Z-D
26. Beth El Y-E
27. Gibeon Y-E
28. Latrun Y-E
29. Jaffa/Tel Aviv X-D
30. Rishon LeZion X-E
31. Ramla X-E
32. Beit Shemesh Y-E
33. Jerusalem Y-E
34. Jericho Z-E
35. Qumran Z-E
36. Bethlehem Y-E

37. Hebron Y-F
38. Gat X-F
39. Beit Guvrin/Maresha Y-E
40. Lachish X-F
41. Ashdod X-E
42. Ashkelon X-E
43. Gaza X-F
44. Ein Gedi Z-F
45. Masada Z-F
46. Arad Y-F
47. Be'er Sheva X-G
48. Sedom Z-G
49. Avdat Y-H
50. Mitzpeh Ramon Y-H
51. Timna Y-K
52. Eilat Y-K

SCALE MAP OF ISRAEL AND THE GOLAN

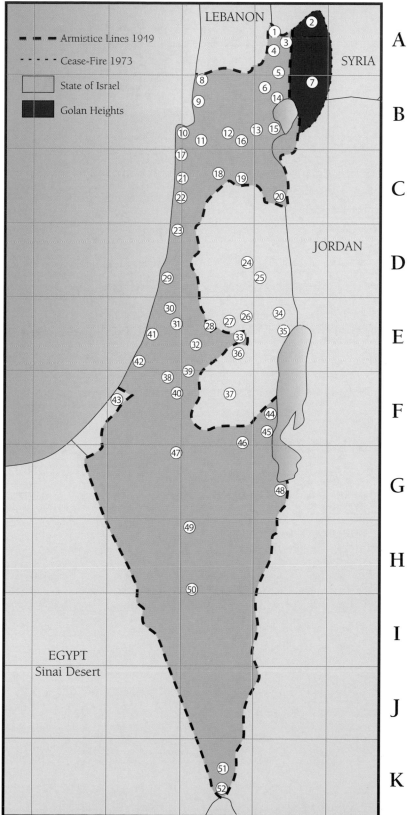

Prehistory to Middle Bronze Age

c. 1800 BCE

The first chapter of Genesis tells the story of the Creation. Modern scientific studies in physics, geology, cosmology, etc., elaborate, confirm or contest this concise explanation of the beginning of everything.

"In the beginning God created the heaven and the earth."

Gen 1:1

The opening words of the Book of Genesis, which in Hebrew is called "Be-Reshit" – "In the beginning"

Traveling the length of the country one can savor the geological splendors and contrasts. Going through the Ramon Machtesh, the strata of the formation of the Earth's crust are exposed in all their beauty. In Timna Park, erosion has created the magnificent pillars, sometimes incorrectly called Solomon's Pillars.

Opposite page: "The Carpentry Shop" in the Ramon Crater is a natural rock formation shaped over time by various pressures into ribbed, symmetrical columns

"And God said, Let the waters under the heaven be gathered together unto one place, and let the dry land appear: and it was so. And God called the dry land Earth; and the gathering together of the waters called He Seas: and God saw that it was good."

Gen 1:9-10

Chemicals in the soil have added color contrasts, as in the Red Canyon. Earth movement, which causes destructive earthquakes, also created waterfalls, such as the chimney near Metullah. The rounded hills of the Golan are extinct volcanoes which spewed out lava — today the black basalt rock.

In the 1930s, in order to build the port of Haifa, extensive quarrying was begun in the Carmel Mountain range. How fortunate that sharp eyes detected the caves of prehistoric man before they were destroyed. Molluscs fossilized into the rocks indicate the chang-

Left: Cave drawing from Mitzpeh Ramon museum garden
Below: Natufian burial site in Carmel mountains

קבורה נטופית (העתק)
NATUFIAN BURIAL (COPY)

Dolmen in
the Golan

ing level of the sea. When pre-historic man used these caves, he could almost cast his fishing line from the cave entrance.

Early man was a nomad, constantly moving, searching for his food — the animals that he hunted. When he realized that not only could he eat some of the things that grow, but could plant and reap and be the master of some of his food requirements, he began the process of settling down.

At the beginning of the century the agronomist Aaron Aaronsohn proved that it was in this area that wild wheat was first domesticated — without even knowing that prehistoric man lived here.

With the process of settling down we enter the Stone Age, so called because man began to use tools — made of stone. The settlements were probably extended family units and, apart from the tools, very little else remains.

About this time there are signs of burial customs. Bodies were sometimes laid in the fetal position and, more important for research, were buried with ornaments. These were usually shells or stones and, by analyzing the source of these semiprecious stones, one can map the areas covered by trade in those early times.

The burial sites were the earliest stone structures, known as dolmens because of their table-like shape. The Gamla area is dotted with dolmens.

Man's next major stepping stone was when he discovered that some mud, when heated, became hard — the beginning of pottery. The different quality of the pottery, its distinctive shapes and decorations guide the archaeologist in the dating process.

Ancient Jericho

Settlements grew beyond the extended family and urbanization began. Settlements were close to a water source, usually sufficiently elevated to give a clear view of the surrounding area, often on one of the main traveling routes. These same locations will be used again and again over the centuries and will become known as tells.

The traveling routes too, were in constant use and form the basis of the modern road system. The Via Maris was the oldest route from Egypt to the north and from there to the Fertile Crescent, traversing the land of Canaan.

Tuthmose III of Egypt described the route he took to conquer Megiddo about four thousand years ago. Just recently, as the modern road through the same Iron Valley was widened, work had to be delayed in order to conduct excavations on ancient sites found along the way.

Jericho boasts of being the oldest city in the world — eight thousand years old. How do we define a "city"? Why should people have settled there particularly? For our purposes "city" refers to a settlement where there is building other than huts for living in, when someone has assumed leadership and directed the community to build a wall around their encampment, or a storage pit, or a temple.

"His majesty (Thutmose III, c. 1490-1436 BCE — B.R.) ordered a conference with his victorious army, speaking as follows: "That enemy of Kadesh has come and has entered into Megiddo. He is there at this moment. He has gathered to him the princes of every foreign country which had been loyal to Egypt,...their horses and their armies and their people, and he says; 'I shall wait here in Megiddo.' Will ye tell me what is in your hearts?'

"'What is it like to go on this road which becomes so narrow? The foe waiting on the other side is becoming more numerous. Will the vanguard of us be fighting while the rearguard is waiting here (at Tel Iron — B.R.) unable to fight. There are two other roads, one to the east comes out at Ta'anach, the other to the north. Let our victorious army proceed on whichever you choose but do not make us go on that difficult road.'"

"'As Re loves me...my majesty shall proceed on this Aruna road! ...Lest these enemies say: 'Has His Majesty set out on another road because he has become afraid of us?' I will not let my army go forth ahead of my majesty." ...Every man was made aware of his order of march, horse following horse, in single file, while His Majesty was at the head of his army,...exhorting. "Capture ye my victorious army...for the capturing of Megiddo is the capturing of a thousand towns."

"Now everything which his majesty did to this town and to that wretched enemy and his wretched army is recorded day by day by the individual troop commanders."

Adapted from J.B. Pritchard, ed., Ancient Near East Texts Relating to the Old Testsment (Princeton, NJ: Princeton University Press, 1950), 235

The site that was to become Jericho had two advantages: fresh water from natural springs and its proximity to the lowest point on Earth. The springs ensured abundant food, and the lowest place on Earth, the Dead Sea, was the source of salt, without which man cannot survive. Salt was probably one of the first items traded.

About five thousand years ago man discovered that copper and tin could be mined, heated, alloyed and then used to make tools more efficient than those of stone. Thus was born the Bronze Age.

The archaeological excavations at Timna reveal how pits were dug and furnaces built. An analysis of the slag that was left behind indicates the heat in those furnaces. The temple close by was no less important than the furnace, perhaps more so, for one had to pray for safety and to give thanks to the gods.

For the archaeologist, the temple area provides a wealth of information. The figurines of the gods, the altars, and perhaps even the remains of the sacrifices, help tell a story about ancient man.

Much of our knowledge of this period comes to us from excavations of tells, such as Megiddo, Lachish, Hatzor and Dan. What is a tell?

Take a small hill close to a water source. Build a few mud houses on it. Perhaps a wall around them. Burial sites on the slope of the hill. Decades pass. The settlement is deserted — perhaps it was attacked and destroyed, perhaps there was a drought and the people moved. Dust and sand cover everything.

"And Joshua at that time turned back, and took Hazor, and smote the king thereof ith a sword: for Hazor beforetime was the head of all those kingdoms."   *Josh 11:10*

Aerial view of Tel Megiddo

Middle Bronze gateway at Tel Dan

More decades pass. New people build on the ruins. Once again the tell is deserted and rebuilt. Stone buildings instead of mud brick. Thicker walls. A massive gateway. A larger temple area. Again destruction — rebuilding. Dust and sand cover each layer.

This time a different style of gateway. Casemate instead of solid walls. Slowly the little hill grows in height. The final destruction and then it will be covered with dust, dirt and maybe even bushes, or will slowly erode, until a twentieth-century archaeologist realizes what lies buried in the hill.

Many tells, including those mentioned above, have over twenty identifiable levels. Some, like Arad, are less complicated and have only a few levels. Deciphering the artifacts and buildings found in each level adds to our knowledge of the ancient periods.

Positive dating is difficult. Carbon-14 testing has a margin of error of about two hundred years and so is only viable when finds are Stone Age and earlier. For later periods, artifacts are correlated with those found in neighboring areas, such as Egypt, the Fertile Crescent, Asia Minor and the Greek Islands, where there is often an agreed-upon chronology and dating.

The land of Canaan was not a country with a central ruler. It was made up of many city-states, sometimes allied with one another, sometimes at war, sometimes allied with Egypt, sometimes with the kingdoms of Mesopotamia. It was a land bridge connecting Africa, Europe and Asia, through which the armies of Egypt, of the kingdoms of the Fertile Crescent and the kingdoms of Asia Minor had to pass on their campaigns of military expansion.

Pharaohs and kings listed the Canaanite cities they conquered in the battle annals engraved on their temples. Based on their geographical and topographical descriptions, archaeologists are able to identify such cities as Dan, Hatzor, Lachish, Megiddo and Arad, to name a few.

After the conquest of the land of Canaan by the Israelites, this area became known as the Kingdom of Israel. As we continue from period to period, we will follow the various name changes that occur.

The following table should help to connect historical events to archaeological periods.

DATE (BCE)	PERIOD	KEY HISTORICAL EVENTS & SITES
250,000-10,000	Paleolithic	Early Stone Age, development of man, Carmel caves
10,000-8,000	Mesolithic	Middle Stone Age, settlements
8,000-4,000	Neolithic	New Stone Age, domestication of animals, ceramic pottery, beginning of urbanization
4,000-3,150	Chalcolithic	Copper and Stone Age, use of copper, hieroglyphic script in Egypt, cuneiform in Mesopotamia
3,150-2,200	Early Bronze	Kingdoms of Accad, Sumer, pyramids in Egypt, fortified Canaanite cities, Arad, Hatzor, Megiddo
2,200-1,550	Middle Bronze	Hammurabi, Mari and Ebla archives, Hyksos in Egypt, palaces of Greece and Troy, Patriarchs, Joseph
1,550-1,200	Late Bronze	Egyptian campaigns in Canaan, El Amarna, Ugarit, Mycenia, Israelites slaves in Egypt, Moses

GENERAL INTRODUCTION Hebrew Scriptures

The Hebrew Scriptures, also known as the Old Testament, are a major source of information for events that took place in the land of Canaan and then in the Kingdoms of Israel and Judah. Inscriptions uncovered in archaeological excavations throughout the ancient Near East are another.

We are going to travel with the Scriptures, dwelling not on the religious, moral or universal message, but wandering along its chronological path, for that is the path this book follows

In Hebrew, the Scriptures are known as "Tanach" (ta-na-ch), a word made up of three consonants just as the Tanach itself is made up of three separate sections. These are: 1) Torah (ta), the Pentateuch; 2) Neviim (na), Prophets; 3) K'tuvim (ch), the Writings.

The Torah consists of Genesis, Exodus, Leviticus, Numbers and Deuteronomy, traditionally given to Moses on Mount Sinai. Some Bible critics doubt this, believing that the books evolved over an extended period. There is no consensus for the disputed dating of any of the five books or their canonization.

Starting with the story of the creation, the Torah continues with the evolution of the descendants of Abraham to become the Israelite people and ends with the death of Moses.

It includes the 613 mitzvot or commandments, which the Israelite nation, and later the Jewish people, are exhorted to obey. It also details the Jewish holy days. One of the fifty-three portions into which it is divided is read every Shabbat (Sabbath).

The Books of Joshua, Judges, Samuel I and II and Kings I and II were considered by the sages to have been written by a prophet, so together with Isaiah, Jeremiah, Ezekiel and the twelve minor prophets they make up the section headed "the Prophets."

The canonization of "the Prophets" is generally thought to have taken place circa 200 BCE. Historically, they cover the period from Moses' death to the Babylonian exile after the destruction of the First Temple in 586 BCE.

The last section, K'tuvim, was only finally selected and canonized around 90 CE. The books forming K'tuvim are Psalms, Proverbs, Job, Song of Songs, Ruth, Lamentations, Ecclesiastes, Esther, Daniel, Ezra, Nehemiah and Chronicles I and II.

Ezra and Nehemiah deal with the return of the exiles from Babylon and the beginning of the Second Temple period. Chronicles detail the genealogy and history from Adam to the declaration of Cyrus of Persia allowing the rebuilding of the Temple in Jerusalem.

In the Christian version of the Old Testament, these books appear in a slightly different order. The Tanach was translated into Greek probably sometime in the third century BCE by seventy translators. Known as the Septuagint, it included the Apocrypha (from the Greek word meaning hidden).

The Apocrypha contains fifteen books, including the first and second books of the Maccabees, which relate to the Jewish revolt against Greek-Seleucid rule, 165-162 BCE. These books were available when K'tuvim was canonized in the first century CE, but were omitted. The Greek Orthodox and other Eastern Churches use the Septuagint and retain the Apocrypha.

The archaeological site of Qumran

"**N**ow these are the names of the children of Israel, which came into Egypt; every man and his household came with Jacob."

The opening words of the Book of Exodus, which in Hebrew is called Shemot, "names"

"**A**nd the Lord called unto Moses, and spake unto him out of the tabernacle of the congregation...."

The opening words of the Book of Leviticus, which in Hebrew is called Va-Yikra, "He called"

"**A**nd the Lord spake unto Moses in the wilderness of Sinai...."

The opening words of the Book of Numbers, which in Hebrew is called Be-Midbar, "in the wilderness"

"**T**hese be the words which Moses spake unto all Israel...."

The opening words of the Book of Deuteronomy, which in Hebrew is called Devarim, "words"

The Vulgate, the Latin translation of the Hebrew Scriptures, and the Greek Septuagint by Hieronymus (St. Jerome) in the fourth century, were the basis for the best-known English version, the King James Bible. Since then, there have been many and varied translations. The early Catholic Church excluded the Apocrypha but reversed this decision at the Council of Trent in 1546. From the beginning of the Reformation in the sixteenth century, the Protestant Churches retained the Apocrypha.

The Dead Sea Scrolls include the earliest known biblical manuscripts and are generally dated first century BCE – first century CE. Every book of the Tanach (Hebrew Scriptures) excluding the Book of Esther is

A portion of the Dead Sea Scrolls

represented. Some are complete and are in an excellent state of preservation, such as the Isaiah scroll. Others are merely fragments. Almost all of these books (each was actually a scroll, written on a long, rolled parchment made of animal hides) were written in Hebrew.

The Apocrypha are represented, as well as hitherto unknown wisdom literature and commentaries. Three unique scrolls, generally known as the Temple Scroll, the Manual of Discipline and the War Scroll (which refers to "the sons of light" and "the sons of darkness") shed light on the philosophy and customs of the Dead Sea sects, including perhaps the Essenes.

Now, let us continue on our journey.

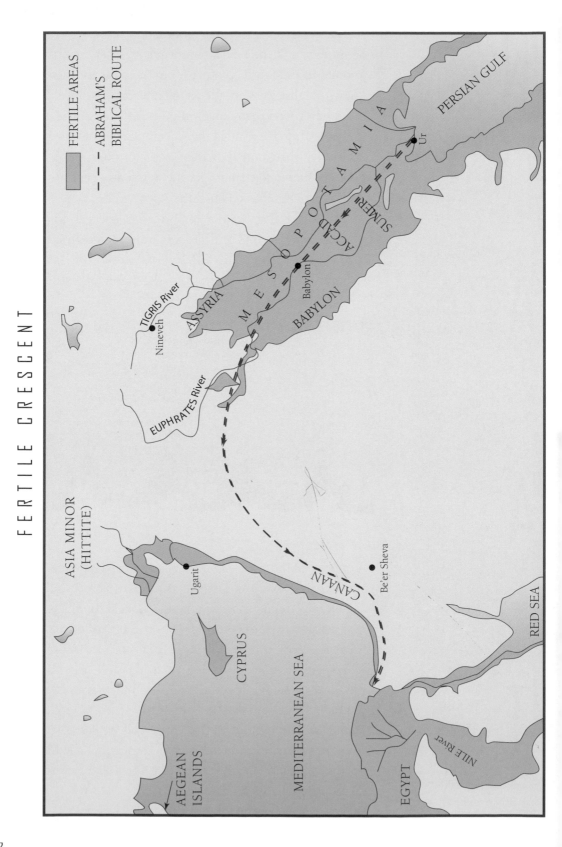

FERTILE CRESCENT

FERTILE AREAS

ABRAHAM'S BIBLICAL ROUTE

PERSIAN GULF

MESOPOTAMIA

SUMER

ACCAD

Ur

Babylon

BABYLON

ASSYRIA

TIGRIS River

Nineveh

EUPHRATES River

ASIA MINOR (HITTITE)

Ugarit

CANAAN

Be'er Sheva

CYPRUS

MEDITERRANEAN SEA

AEGEAN ISLANDS

EGYPT

NILE River

RED SEA

c. 3800 to c. 1200 BCE

Torah: Abraham to Moses

The biblical stories in Genesis cannot be definitely dated but are usually placed in the archaeological period known as the MB (Middle Bronze Age, 1800 to 1600 BCE).

Abraham was born in Ur, at the head of the Persian Gulf. He wandered along the Fertile Crescent to the land known as Canaan, where he settled in the plains around Hebron. His nephew Lot settled in the Jordan Valley, near Sodom, one of the five cities in the fertile plain at the southern end of the Dead Sea.

Rock formation on Mount Sodom

"**N**ow the Lord had said unto Abram, Get thee out of thy country, and from thy kindred, and from thy father's house, unto a land that I will shew thee: And I will make of thee a great nation, and I will bless thee, and make thy name great; and thou shalt be a blessing: And I will bless them that bless thee, and curse him that curseth thee: and in thee shall all families of the earth be blessed."

Gen 12:1-3

> "**T**hen the Lord rained upon Sodom and upon Gomorrah brimstone and fire from the Lord out of heaven."
> *Gen 19:24*

The biblical narrative tells us that Sodom and its neighbor, Gomorrah, were evil cities and were going to be destroyed by God. Lot managed to flee but was told not to look back. His wife did — and was turned into a pillar of salt.

Archaeological excavations show us that the southern tip of the Dead Sea was fertile, well fed by natural springs and populated. All this was destroyed and the area remained desolate almost up to present times. Today hundreds of thousands of tourists visit there annually.

Thanks to a unique combination of sulphur springs, richly oxygenated air and filtered sun rays (this being the lowest place on earth, 400 m or 1300 ft. below sea level) this area is endowed with therapeutic properties.

Sufferers from psoriasis and other skin diseases, as well as from rheumatic pains, take the cure at the many hotels along the Dead Sea coast. The healthy enjoy the sensation of floating on the water and being covered with the black mud.

Various views of the Dead Sea

Three times God blessed Abraham: "I will make of thee a great nation and I will bless thee" (Gen 12:2); "unto thy seed will I give this land" (Gen 12:7); "Arise, walk through the land in the length of it and in the breadth of it; for I will give it unto thee" (Gen 13:17).

But his wife Sarah was barren. Ishmael was born of the handmaiden Hagar. Due to Sarah's jealousy they were cast out into the Sinai Desert where, according to tradition, Ishmael became the ancestor of the Bedouin tribes of the southern desert.

Finally Sarah, in her old age, gave birth to Isaac. Abraham and his family lived in the arid Negev in the vicinity of Be'er Sheva, by whose wells he and Abimelech swore a pact of friendship.

Abraham's faith in one God was put to the test when he was told "Take now thy son, thine only son Isaac, whom thou lovest, and get thee into the land of Moriah; and offer him there for a burnt offering upon one of the mountains which I will tell thee of" (Gen 22:2).

Mount Moriah, where Abraham, ready to sacrifice Isaac, instead sacrificed a ram that was caught in the thicket, is traditionally identified as the place where the First and Second Temples to the God of Israel were built, and where, today, the Dome of the Rock stands.

> I will give thee money for the field; take it of me, and I will bury my dead there. And Ephron answered Abraham, saying unto him,...the land is worth four hundred shekels of silver...and Abraham weighed to Ephron the silver..."
>
> *Gen 23:13-16*

When Sarah died, Abraham purchased from Ephron the Hittite a field and cave at Mamre, the Cave of Machpela in Hebron, where he buried her. Here he too was buried, as were his son Isaac and wife Rebecca, their son Jacob and his wife, Leah. (Rachel, another of Jacob's wives, is buried at Bethlehem.) Collectively they are known as the Patriarchs and Matriarchs.

Cave of Machpela in Hebron, burial place of the Patriarchs and Matriarchs

Isaac and Rebecca spent most of their life in the arid Negev. Their son Jacob, who deceived his father Isaac by dressing as his twin brother Esau thereby receiving the blessing meant for Esau (Gen 27:27-29), fled to Haran, to his mother's brother Laban.

There he fell in love with Rachel but was tricked into marrying her older sister Leah. Fourteen years he worked for his uncle Laban, to pay for both wives.

On his return to Canaan he wrestled with the angel, prevailed, and his name was changed to Israel. From this point the story of the patriarchal family widens to become the story of the children of Israel

Abraham's Well in Be'er Sheva

"And he said, Thy name shall be called no more Jacob, but Israel: for as a prince hast thou power with God and with men, and hast prevailed."
Gen 32:29

evolving into a nation. The descendants of the twelve sons of Jacob/Israel will become the twelve tribes of Israel.

One of the sons, Joseph, was sold into slavery by his jealous brothers. After many trials and tribulations and successes in deciphering dreams, he rose to the rank of the second most powerful man in Egypt, after the Pharaoh. As such, he was able to offer hospitality to his family, fleeing from famine in the land of Canaan.

On his deathbed, Jacob blessed his own sons and the two sons of Joseph. These blessings are beautifully depicted in the twelve stained glass windows by Marc Chagall in the synagogue of the Hadassah Hospital in Jerusalem.

At this point the book of Genesis comes to an end and the story of the descendants of Jacob/Israel continues in Exodus.

On their arrival, Joseph's family were made welcome in Egypt but over the decades, and perhaps even centuries, their descendants became slaves. Under the leadership of Moses they were led out of Egypt.

Burial place of Rachel in Bethlehem

"I am the Lord thy God...[;] Thou shalt have no other gods before Me. Thou shalt not make unto thee any graven image...[;] Thou shalt not take the name of the Lord thy God in vain...[;] Remember the Sabbath day, to keep it holy...[;] Honor thy father and thy mother...[;] Thou shalt not kill[;] Thou shalt not commit adultery[;] Thou shalt not steal[;] Thou shalt not bear false witness...[;] Thou shalt not covet any thing that is thy neighbor's."

Ex 20:2-14

There is no agreed dating for the Exodus from Egypt. Most researchers place it in the thirteenth century BCE. No Pharaoh left for posterity the ignominious detail that during his reign the Israelite slaves departed, so we have no Egyptian sources to help in precise dating.

The location of Mount Sinai, where Moses received the tablets of the law, has not been positively identified, nor has the route of forty years of wandering in the desert. However, the Ten Commandments, given to Moses, are as valid today as they were then.

The laws in the books of Exodus, Leviticus, Numbers and Deuteronomy are the laws that will guide the children of Israel for the next three thousand years. Broadly speaking, they define man's relationship with God, with man and with nature.

Many laws and customs of the modern world first appeared in the Torah. To cite but a few at random: a day of rest from work on the seventh day; allowing fields to lie fallow (the seventh year); taking care of our sick and our elderly; planting a tree to replace that which we cut down. Other codes of law that existed at this time were not as comprehensive and did not recognize the equality of all before the law.

The Holy Days, including the Shabbat and the three Pilgrimage Festivals, Pesach (Passover), Shavuot (Weeks) and Succot (Tabernacles) were defined.

Deuteronomy, and the Torah, end with the death of Moses. He blessed the tribes and then went to Mount Nevo to gaze at the Promised Land, to which he was denied entry. He died and was buried "but no man knoweth his sepulchre" (Deut 34:6).

Although the use of bronze tools continues while the use of iron spreads gradually, archaeologically the Bronze Age now ends and the next period will be the Iron Age, also known as the Israelite period.

Hikers approaching the summit of Mount Sinai

ALLOCATIONS OF ISRAELITE TRIBES
13TH-12TH CENTURIES BCE

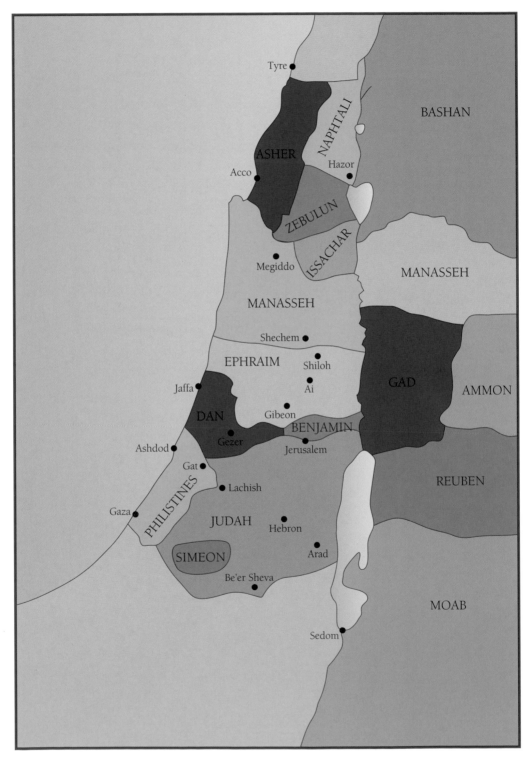

CHAPTER 4

1200-56 BCE Israelite Period

Our sources for this period, in addition to archaeological excavations, are the Books of Joshua, Judges, Samuel, Kings and the various prophets. The major historical divisions are:

1200-1020 BCE	Israelite conquest of Canaan
1020-928 BCE	Saul, David, Solomon
928-721 BCE	Kingdoms of Israel and Judah
721-586 BCE	Kingdom of Judah

Just as there is controversy about the dating of the Exodus, so too is there controversy about the conquest. Was it a rapid process, a slow infiltration, or a mixture of both?

As we have mentioned, the land of Canaan was not a unified country with a central ruler but consisted of many "city-states" each ruled by its own king. At this time, Egypt was in one of her weaker periods and the Canaanite kings were free from foreign domination.

The meandering Jordan River

The Book of Joshua, as its name implies, relates specifically to Joshua and his deeds. Traditions relating to the tribes in general are preserved in the Book of Judges. Both tell of the battles of the conquest. Perhaps there were other sources which have been lost.

Under the leadership of Joshua, the waters of the Jordan River parted to allow the children of Israel to cross (as the Red Sea had parted for Moses).

Tel Lachish

The first city to be conquered was Jericho, whose "walls fell down flat" (Josh 6:20).

Archaeologists have not as yet identified any walls or remains that can be dated to this period and there are those who cast doubt as to the accuracy of this account of the conquest of Jericho.

Ai, Lachish, Gezer, Hebron and Debir fell to the invading Israelites, completing the conquest in the south. In the north, the kingdoms allied with Hazor were routed.

Joshua called a convocation, erected an altar on Mount Ebal where sacrifices were offered, and read out to the assembled people the laws given to Moses.

Many of the sites mentioned have been excavated, some identified. The archaeological interpretations of the dating of the walls and buildings and of destruction levels often do not tally with the dating given to the biblical story. Archaeologists debate with one another, as do biblical historians and scholars, sometimes vehemently.

At Shiloh the land was divided amongst the tribes, two and one half tribes on the east bank of the Jordan, nine and one half on the west bank (Josh 13-21).

The description of the Na'hala (inheritance) of each tribe included geographical and topographical details, distances between towns (tells) and their proximity to rivers and mountains. All this taken together helps to identify the many tells dotted about the country. Not always foolproof, but certainly indicative.

The Book of Judges, which covers the period between 1200 BCE and 1040 BCE, starts by listing all the towns not taken by the tribes in their respective areas.

They live among the various Canaanite peoples — Hittites, Amorites, Perizites, Hivites, Jebusites. When they forsook God, "The anger of the Lord was hot against Israel, and He...sold them into the hands of their enemies...." But then "The Lord raised up judges, which delivered them...." (Judg 2:14, 16).

"**T**hen sang Deborah and Barak.... Hear, O ye kings; give ear, O ye princes; I, even I, will sing unto the Lord; I will sing praise to the Lord God of Israel.... The kings came and fought, then fought the kings of Canaan in Taanach by the waters of Megiddo.... The river of Kishon swept them away, that ancient river, the river Kishon."

Judges 5:1, 3, 19, 21

This is the message throughout the Book of Judges.

The first judges, Othniel, Ehud ben Gera and Shamgar, are only briefly mentioned. The story of Deborah, wife of Lapidoth, is given in greater detail (chapters 4 and 5).

Together with her general, Barak, Deborah battled against Jabin of Hazor and his captain, Sisera. On the banks of the Kishon River, at the foot of Megiddo, the Canaanite chariots were bogged down in the mud, thereby facilitating an Israelite victory. Sisera escaped but was killed by Yael.

The story of Gideon, the next judge, is long and replete with geographical details. At the springs of Ein Harod, Gideon chose an army of three hundred out of the thousands who had volunteered and, using surprise tactics, routed the Midianites (chapters 6-8).

Jezréel Valley

One of his seventy sons, Abimelech, mothered by a Canaanite woman ("for Gideon had many wives"), was ambitious. He killed all his brothers (except one, Jotham, who escaped), and set himself up as King of Shechem, which he eventually destroyed (chapter 9).

Most archaeologists agree that one of the conflagration levels at Shechem could

"**T**hen Jerubbaal, who is Gideon, and all the people that were with him, rose up early, and pitched beside the well of Harod:... And the Lord said unto Gideon, The people are yet too many; bring them down unto the water, and I will try them.... Every one that lappeth of the water with his tongue, as a dog lappeth, him shalt thou set by himself; likewise every one that boweth down upon his knees to drink.... By the three hundred men that lapped will I save you, and deliver the Midianites into thine hand."

Judges 7:1, 4, 5, 7

be dated to this event in the twelfth century BCE.

Other judges were Tola, Yair, Yiftach, Ivtzan, Eilon, Abdon and, finally, the last — Samson of Zorah. Many were his escapades. With Delilah of Sorek, Samson finally met his downfall. His hair, source of his strength, was shorn, and he was taken prisoner to Gaza where his eyes were gored out. But the final word was his.

Tied between the two main pillars of the temple in Gaza, he cried, "Let me die with the Philistines," as he brought their temple down about his head (chapters 13-16).

The Book of Samuel covers the years circa 1040 BCE to 970 BCE and starts with the birth of Samuel and his dedication to Eli the priest at Shiloh (which is where the ark of the covenant was kept in a tabernacle).

The Israelites at Eben Ezer were battling the Philistines at Aphek and were losing. The ark brought from Shiloh to protect them was captured by the Philistines, who took it to Ashdod.

Fearful that the presence of the ark was responsible for the destruction of the statue of Dagon, the Philistines, of Ashdod sent the ark to their compatriots in Gat. When disaster struck there too, it was passed to the Philistines of Ekron (all three were Philistine cities) but the people of Ekron did not want it.

On the advice of their prophets the Philistines placed the ark on a new cart which was hitched to oxen that had never worn a yoke, and then set it free (I Samuel 5 and 6). The oxen made directly for the Israelite town of Beit Shemesh. From there the ark was moved to Kiryat Yearim, there to remain until brought to its permanent resting place in Jerusalem.

The pressure of the Philistines continued and the people appealed to Samuel to "Make us a king to judge us like all nations." Samuel tried to dis-

> "The Philistines took him, and put out his eyes, and brought him down to Gaza.... Then the lords of the Philistines gathered them together for to offer a great sacrifice unto Dagon their god.... And they called for Samson out of the prison house;... and they set him between the pillars.... And Samson took hold of the two middle pillars upon which the house stood.... And Samson said, Let me die with the Philistines. And he bowed himself with all his might; and the house fell upon the lords."
>
> *Judges 16:21-30*

suade them but they wanted their king to "Judge us and go out before us and fight our battles" (I Samuel 8).

Samuel annointed Saul, whose twenty-year reign was one of war, mainly against the Philistines. Saul would not be the forerunner of a dynasty.

Archaeology has enriched our knowledge of the Philistines. They were one of the Sea People, and the only ones who really left their mark. They reached Canaan in the twelfth century BCE, about the same time as the Aegean kingdoms, including Crete, disintegrated. The tomb of Rameses III depicts a sea battle between the Egyptians and the invading Sea People. The event is generally dated 1177 BCE.

The Sea People did not conquer Egypt but settled along the southern coast of Canaan, whether as vassals of Egypt or allies defending her southern border, we cannot be sure. In excavations, a definite Philistine culture can be detected. The Philistines had the knowledge to make iron, as yet unknown to the Israelites. This knowledge gave them a military advantage, as well as better agricultural tools.

The waterfall at Ein Gedi

The Philistines will eventually be overpowered by David and thereafter play a minor role until their total disappearance by the eighth century BCE.

Between Sochoh and Azeka, separated by the Elah Valley, the Israelites and Philistines faced one another. Here it was that David felled Goliath with a river pebble and a sling (I Samuel 15).

"Now the Philistines gathered together their armies to battle...between Sochoh and Azekah.... And Saul and the men of Israel were gathered together...by the valley of Elah.... And there went out a champion out of the camp of the Philistines.... And all the men of Israel...were sore afraid.... And David... took his staff in his hand, and chose him five smooth stones out of the brook, and put them in a shepherd's bag which he had,...and his sling was in his hand....

"And David put his hand in his bag, and took thence a stone, and slang it, and smote the Philistine in his forehead...and he fell upon his face.... David ran, and...took his sword, and drew it out of the sheath thereof, and slew him, and cut off his head therewith. And when the Philistines saw their champion was dead, they fled."

I Sam 17:1-51

Aerial view of Beit Shean showing the ancient tell and the Roman city below

David, and Saul's son, Jonathan, became firm friends. Because of Saul's jealousy, David was forced to flee to the caves of Ein Gedi and eventually took refuge with Achish, one of the Philistine kings.

When the Philistines were once more poised for battle against the Israelites, Achish, unsure of David's loyalty, told David to leave, thereby saving him from the dilemma of what to do if called upon to attack the Israelites.

The Israelites were defeated and Saul's sons were killed. When Saul's body was discovered by the Philistines it was mutilated and displayed on the walls of Beit Shean. The men of Jabesh Gilead retrieved his body and gave him and his sons a decent burial (I Samuel 31).

David's magnificent lamentation for Saul and Jonathan ends one period, the reign of Saul, and opens the next, the reign of David.

"The men of Judah came, and there they anointed David King over the house of Judah..." (II Samuel 2:4), and for the first seven and a half years he ruled from Hebron.

"Thy glory, O Israel, is slain upon thy high places: how are the mighty fallen! Tell it not in Gath, publish it not in the streets of Ashkelon; lest the daughters of the Philistines rejoice.... Ye mountains of Gilboa, let there be no dew, neither let there be rain, upon you, nor fields of offerings: for there the shield of the mighty is vilely cast away, the shield of Saul, as though he had not been anointed with oil. From the blood of the slain, from the fat of the mighty, the bow of Jonathan turned not back, and the sword of Saul returned not empty. Saul and Jonathan were lovely and pleasant in their lives, and in their death they were not divided: they were swifter than eagles, they were stronger than lions. Ye daughters of Israel, weep over Saul, who clothed you in scarlet, with other delights, who put on ornaments of gold upon your apparel. How are the mighty fallen in the midst of the battle!"

II Sam 1:19-25

With the conquest of Jebus, captured when Yoav ben Zuriah "getteth up to the gutter" (II Samuel 5:8; perhaps a hint that he gained control of the water supply of the city, causing the people to surrender), the capital now became Jerusalem, City of David.

The final chapter of the book of Samuel tells of David's defiance in taking a population census. To lift the plague that this caused, David was told to purchase the threshing ground of Arouna and there to build an altar and make a sacrifice to God.

> "Nay; but I will surely buy it of thee at a price: neither will I offer burnt offerings unto the Lord my God of that which doth cost me nothing. So David bought the threshing floor and the oxen for fifty shekels of silver. And David built there an altar unto the Lord, and offered burnt offerings and peace offerings."
>
> II Sam 24:24-25

Arouna offered the land as a gift but David insisted on paying a fair price. The deed of sale for the piece of land on which David built an altar — and his son Solomon built the Temple — is recorded in II Samuel 24:24 and I Chronicles 21:24. (Traditionally, this is the same spot where Abraham prepared an altar to sacrifice Isaac.)

The Temple built by Solomon will stand over four hundred years, will be destroyed by the Babylonians but very shortly will be rebuilt. The Second Temple, in use for over five hundred years, will be destroyed by the Romans in 70 CE.

During David's rule the kingdom was strengthened and enlarged. As he lay dying, the fight for the succession began. Adonijah appeared to have taken over the reins but Nathan the Prophet and Bath-sheba reminded David of his promise that Solomon would reign after his death. David instructed Zadok the priest to anoint Solomon at the Gihon spring.

So ends David's rule, which is generally dated circa 1000 BCE to 961 BCE.

Solomon's first act was to consolidate the kingdom. Then, using the iron and cedar, gold and silver prepared by David, Solomon spent seven years building the Temple. He was advised by Hiram the Phoenician, a master builder. The Temple is described in great detail but no archaeological remains have been uncovered.

We are told that Solomon fortified Hazor, Megiddo and Gezer. Professor Yigal Yadin, excavator of Hazor, describes the discovery of what he believed to be Solomon's gates:

Excavation of City of David

View of Jerusalem from the Haas Promenade. In the foreground is the outline of the City of David. To the right the Kidron Valley. In the center the Southern Wall of the Old City, built by Suleiman II c. 1537. Above it is the Dome of the Rock, which is on Mount Moriah, site of the First and Second Temples.

To impress our laborers, even before the contours and plan of the gate become clear, we traced the plan of the Megiddo gates [already excavated — B.R.] on the ground, marking it with pegs to denote corners and walls and then instructed them to dig according to the marking, promising "here you will find a wall" or "there you will find a chamber."

When our prophecies proved correct our prestige went up enormously... when we read the biblical verse about Solomon's activities in Hazor, Megiddo and Gezer, our prestige took a dive but that of the Scriptures rose sky-high!

Solomon and the Queen of Sheba exchanged gifts and opened up a trade route to the east coast of Africa via the port of Ezion Geber — Eilat of today. Ethiopian tradition holds that Menelik, the founder of the Ethiopian dynasty, was the son the Queen of Sheba bore to Solomon. The emperors of Ethiopia, up until Haile Selassie in the twentieth century CE, were known as "Lion of Judah," among their other titles.

Solomon was a wise king with a weakness for women — seven hundred wives and three hundred concubines. Many of the marriages were out of political expedience, to cement alliances with Moab, Ammon, Edom, Zidon and the Hittites. The freedom he granted to worship pagan gods angered God. Solomon's descendants would not rule the northern tribes of Israel (I Kings 11:11-13).

In fact the seeds for the division of the kingdom were sown during Solomon's reign. Jeroboam, son of Nebat, had been appointed the overseer of the royal building projects. As his power grew, so too did his appetite.

He was encouraged by the prophet Ahijah of Shiloh, who assured him that God had promised that the descendants of Solomon would not rule the ten tribes of Israel, but that he, Jeroboam, would.

When Solomon learned of this plot, Jeroboam was forced to flee to Egypt, where he was offered shelter by Shishak.

Upon Solomon's death, his son, Rehoboam, went to Shechem, to be proclaimed king. The northern tribes sent representatives to voice their grievances. Instead of following the advice given to him by the elders who had served Solomon, Rehoboam threatened to be even more demanding than his father.

Angered, the people of Israel called upon Jeroboam to be their king. Thus, the kingdom created by David and consolidated by Solomon ceased to exist. The separate kingdoms of Judah and Israel came into being.

The beginning of the reigns of Rehoboam and Jeroboam

Southwestern corner of the Temple Mount, with the inscription from Isaiah (66:10) "Rejoice ye with Jerusalem, and be glad with her, all ye that love her: rejoice with her, all ye that mourn for her." In the foreground the excavated remains of Umayyad palace.

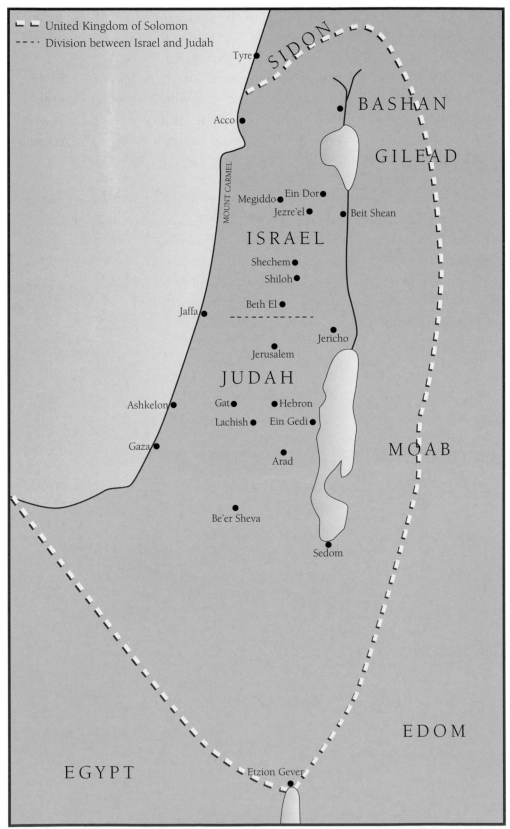

SOLOMON'S KINGDOM

- ⌐ ⌐ United Kingdom of Solomon
- - - - Division between Israel and Judah

SIDON

Tyre

BASHAN

Acco

GILEAD

MOUNT CARMEL

Megiddo · Ein Dor
Jezre'el · · Beit Shean

ISRAEL

Shechem ·
Shiloh ·

Beth El ·

Jaffa ·

Jericho ·

Jerusalem ·

JUDAH

Ashkelon ·   Gat · · Hebron
Lachish · Ein Gedi ·

Gaza ·

MOAB

Arad ·

Be'er Sheva ·

Sedom ·

EDOM

EGYPT

Etzion Gever

is generally accepted as 922 BCE. The northern kingdom of Israel will exist for two hundred years; the kingdom of Judah for 336. During those periods, Israel had nineteen kings; Judah had nineteen kings and one queen.

The following table shows when each ruled and who the neighboring ruler was. Because the Scriptures were not meant to be a history book, there are no definite dates to indicate the beginning or the end of a rule. Setting dates is a matter of analysis, comparisons and deductions. Biblical scholars are not always in agreement so do not be alarmed if you have a book that gives slightly different dates.

KINGS OF JUDAH		KINGS OF ISRAEL		PROPHETS
928-911	Rehoboam	928-906	Jeroboam	
911-908	Abijam	907-906	Nadav	
908-867	Asa	906-883	Baasha	
		883-882	Elah	
		882-882	Zimri	
		882-871	Omri	
867-846	Jehoshaphat	871-852	Ahab	Elijah
		852-851	Ahaziah	
846-843	Jehoram	851-842	Jehoram	
843-842	Ahaziah			
842-836	Athalia	842-814	Jehu	
		814-800	Jehoahaz	
836-798	Joash	800-784	Jehoash	
798-769	Amaziah	784-784	Jeroboam II	Amos (c. 760-?)
769-733	Uzziah	748-748	Zecharia	Josea (c. 740-20)
		748-748	Shallum	
758-743	Jotham	747-737	Menahem	
		737-735	Pekahiah	
		735-733	Pekah	
733-727	Ahaz	733-724	Hoshea	
727-698	Hezekiah			Isaiah (c. 710-?)
698-642	Manasseh			Nahum (c. 650)
641-640	Amon			Zephaniah, Micah, Jonah
640-609	Josiah			Jeremiah (c. 626-586)
609-609	Jehoahaz			
609-598	Jehoiakim			Habakkuk
597-597	Jehoiachin			
596-586	Zedekiah			Ezekiel (c. 600-580)

The size of the two kingdoms depended on the varying strength of the kings of Judah and Israel and of their neighbors.

Judah was the more stable. All the kings were of the Davidian dynasty, Jerusalem was the capital and the Temple was the center of religious life. However, Judah was the smaller and poorer of the two.

Israel comprised the area of the ten tribes, including the eastern side of the Jordan River. Control of the coastal area meant trade and the fertile land meant abundant agriculture. Changing dynasties meant political unrest.

To strengthen his ties with the seafaring Phoenicians, Ahab, heir to Omri, married Jezebel daughter of the king of Sidon. She was instrumental in spreading the cults of Baal and Ashtoreth causing the prophet Elijah to proclaim: "As the Lord God of Israel liveth...there shall not be dew nor rain these years, but according to my word." With that he fled to Cherith, where he was fed by ravens (I Kings 17:1-6).

His capital moved from Shechem to Penuel, in the Gilead, and then to Tirza. His dynasty ended with the murder of his son, Nadav, by Baasha.

In the third year of the drought he returned to Israel and, brought before Ahab, demanded that the pagan prophets be assembled on Mount Carmel. There he challenged them to what was in reality a confrontation between monotheism and paganism. Who would send fire to consume the sacrifice, the pagan gods or the Lord?

Elijah taunted the pagan prophets as Baal failed to consume the sacrifice (perhaps he is on a journey, or sleepeth and must be awakened),

Statue of the prophet Elijah on Mount Carmel

"And the word of the Lord came to Elijah the Tishbite, saying, Arise, go down to meet Ahab king of Israel...saying, Thus saith the Lord, Hast thou killed, and also taken possession? ...In the place where dogs licked the blood of Naboth shall dogs lick thy blood, even thine.... The dogs shall eat of Jezebel by the wall of Jezreel.'"

I Kings 21:17-23

and as evening fell he prepared his altar and called: "Hear me, oh Lord...that these people might know that Thou art the Lord God" (I Kings 18:19-40).

With that, the sacrifice was consumed. Elijah ordered the remorseful people to kill all the false prophets and told Ahab that the drought was ended. However, he fled to Mount Horev (also known as Mount Sinai), to avoid Jezebel's wrath.

Instructed by God to return, he met Elisha and, by casting his mantle over him, indicated that he was to be his successor.

When Jezebel organized two false witnesses so that Ahab could acquire the vineyards of Navot, which he coveted, Elijah informed him that his dynasty would end with his son's short rule.

Amos

"...Behold, the days come, saith the Lord, that the plowman shall overtake the reaper, and the treader of grapes him that soweth seed; and the mountains shall drop sweet wine, and all the hills shall melt. And I will bring again the captivity of My people of Israel, and they shall build the waste cities, and inhabit them; and they shall plant vineyards, and drink the wine thereof; they shall also make gardens, and eat the fruit of them. And I will plant them upon their land, and they shall no more be pulled up out of their land which I have given them, saith the Lord thy God." 9:13-15

Hosea

"...Yet I am the Lord thy God. ...Therefore I will be unto them as a lion: as a leopard by the way will I observe them: I will meet them as a bear that is bereaved of her whelps, and I will rend the caul of their heart, and there will I devour them like a lion: the wild beast shall tear them. O Israel, thou hast destroyed thyself; for thou hast rebelled against Me, against thine help." 13:4-9

Isaiah

"...Come ye, and let us go up to the mountain of the Lord, to the house of the God of Jacob; and he will teach us of His ways, and we will walk in His paths: for out of Zion shall go forth the law, and the word of the Lord from Jerusalem. And He shall judge among the nations, and shall decide among many people: and they shall beat their swords into plowshares, and their spears into pruning hooks: nation shall not lift up sword against nation, neither shall they learn war any more." 2:3-4

Jeremiah

"...Fear not thou, O my servant Jacob, and be not dismayed, O Israel: for, behold, I will save thee from afar off, and thy seed from the land of their captivity; and Jacob shall return, and be in rest and at ease, and none shall make him afraid. Fear thou not, O Jacob My servant, saith the Lord: for I am with thee; for I will make a full end of all the nations wither I have driven thee: but I will not make a full end of thee, but correct thee in measure; yet I will not leave thee wholly unpunished." 46:27-28

From an Assyrian obelisk showing Jehu kneeling at the feet of Shalmaneser we learn of the Assyrian subjugation of Israel.

Under Jeroboam II of Israel and Uzziah of Judah a period of peace, prosperity and renewed power lasted about forty years. The prophets Amos and Hosea protested the exploitation by the wealthy classes in Israel.

Judah expanded, reaching as far south as Sinai. For his arrogance Uzziah was afflicted with leprosy and was buried outside the royal tomb. The inscribed tombstone originally placed over his grave was found on the Mount of Olives.

The rise of Tiglat Pileser (Pul in the Scriptures) brought once again the almost total subjugation of Israel by Assyria. The destruction wrought by this invasion can be seen in the excavations at Hatzor and Megiddo.

Israel was reduced by Samaria, besieged by Shalmaneser, and in 723 BCE was finally totally vanquished. From an inscription left by Sargon, we learn that most of the population were exiled to other parts of the Assyrian Empire. The descendants of these deportees would come to be known as the ten lost tribes of Israel. The Jews of Ethiopia who, in the 1980s and 1990s all emigrated to the modern Israel, may well be descendants of one of the lost tribes.

As was customary, Assyrian mercenaries and deportees from other conquered areas were moved to Samaria. Together with the Israelites who had not been deported, these would be known as Samaritans.

> ❝ conquered and sacked...Samaria, and all Israel (lit. Omri-land).... I led away as prisoners 27,290 inhabitants.... I rebuilt and settled therein people from countries which I myself had conquered. I placed an officer of mine as governor over them."
>
> *Annals of Sargon II, 721-705 BCE*
> (Pritchard, *Ancient Near Eastern Texts*, 284-86)

> "So was Israel carried away out of their own land to Assyria unto this day. And the king of Assyria brought men from Babylon, and from Cuthah, and from Ava,...and placed them in the cities of Samaria instead of the children of Israel: and they possessed Samaria and dwelt in the cities thereof."
>
> *II Kings 17:23-24*

Judah was temporarily spared the Assyrian assault and Hezekiah set about fortifying his kingdom. In Jerusalem, a tunnel increased the water supply to the city thereby allowing its expansion, as far as the broad wall in the west. Archaeological excavations have revealed the original water system of the Jebusites and the tunnel dug in the eighth century BCE, identified by the inscription found engraved on the wall of the tunnel.

Opposite page: Megiddo — part of the water system originally built by the Canaanites and enlarged during the Israelite period

The Broad Wall, in the Jewish Quarter of the Old City, is from the time of Hezekiah; its discovery was important as it was the first positive indication that biblical Jerusalem expanded well beyond the confines of the City of David

The extent that biblical Jerusalem spread westwards has been confirmed by the discovery and positive dating of the Broad Wall.

"Then the tunnel was driven through. And this was the way in which it was cut through. While...each man [dug] toward his fellow, and while there were still three cubits to be cut through, [there was heard] the voice of a man calling to his fellow, for there was an overlap in the rock.... And when the tunnel was driven through, the quarrymen hewed [the rock], each man towards his fellow, axe against axe; and the water flowed from the spring towards the reservoir."

The Siloam Inscription
Discovered in situ 1880, Istanbul Museum
(Pritchard, *Ancient Near Eastern Texts*, 321)

"As to Hezekiah, the Jew, he did not submit to my yoke. I laid siege to forty-six of his strong cities, walled forts and the countless small villages in their vicinity, and conquered them by means of earth ramps and battering rams..., by attack by foot soldiers using mine, breeches as well as sapper work.... I drove out 200,150 people...and I considered them booty. Himself I made a prisoner in Jerusalem, his royal residence, like a bird in a cage."

Annals of Sennacherib, 704-681 BCE
(Pritchard, *Ancient Near Eastern Texts*, 288)

Taking advantage of a Babylonian revolt against Assyria and against Isaiah's advice, Hezekiah stopped paying tribute to Assyria and organized a coalition against her, together with Egypt.

On the walls of Sennacherib's palace in Nineveh is a list of the towns and villages of Judah that were destroyed by the Assyrians, as well as a relief depicting the storming of Lachish. Jerusalem was under siege but, as prophesied by Isaiah (II Kings 19:7), the Assyrian army departed and Jerusalem was spared from vassalage.

For the next half decade, under Manasseh and Amon, all Hezekiah's religious reforms were forgotten and paganism was rife in Judah. Comprehensive reforms were once more introduced by Josiah, to whom some biblical scholars attribute Deuteronomy.

Babylon and Egypt gained independence from a now weakened Assyria. Josiah tried to block the advance of Egypt towards Assyria and was killed at Megiddo. Judah became a vassal of Egypt, but not for long. The campaigns between Egypt and Babylon continued, each trying to inherit the position of dominance vacated by Assyria.

In 598 BCE Jehoiachin and thousands of his subjects were taken as prisoners by Nebuchadnezzar to Babylon. Under the puppet king Zedekiah, and against the advice of Jeremiah, Judah joined Egypt in a revolt against Babylon.

Retribution wasn't long in coming. Judah was laid waste and Jerusalem was completely destroyed. Once more there were deportations to Babylon. Independent Jewish life in the Holy Land, which was laid waste, virtually came to an end. Paradoxically, it would thrive in Babylon.

A replica of the Ivory Pomegranate from the First Temple Period

"By the rivers of Babylon, there we sat down, yea, we wept, when we remembered Zion. We hanged our harps upon the willows in the midst thereof. For there they that carried us away captive required of us a song; and they that spoiled us required of us mirth, saying, Sing us one of the songs of Zion. How shall we sing the Lord's song in a strange land? If I forget thee, O Jerusalem, let my right hand forget her cunning. If I do not remember thee, let my tongue cleave to the roof of my mouth; if I prefer not Jerusalem above my chief joy."

Psalm 137:1-6

CHAPTER 5

C. 538-70 BCE Second Temple Period

"Then Darius the king made a decree, and search was made in the house of the rolls, where the treasures were laid up in Babylon. And there was found at Achmetha, in the palace that is in the province of the Medes, a roll, and therein was a record thus written: In the first year of Cyrus the king the same Cyrus the king made a decree Concerning the house of God at Jerusalem; let the house be builded, the place where they offered sacrifices, and let the foundations thereof be strongly laid;...and let the expenses be given out of the king's house: And also let the golden and silver vessels of the house of God, which Nebuchadnezzar took forth out of the temple which is at Jerusalem, and brought unto Babylon, be restored, and brought again unto the temple which is at Jerusalem, every one to his place, and place them in the house of God."

Ezra 6:1-5

INTRODUCTION

As the heading implies, this chapter covers the entire period during which the Second Temple stood. Using the more common historical or archaeological terms, this chapter has been subdivided according to the powers which ruled the area.

The Babylonian Empire was superseded by the Persian Empire, which was replaced by the Greek Empire, which in turn was conquered by the Roman Empire. Each of these powers left its imprint. In spite of their seeming invincibility, each one exited from the stage of history, never to return again.

The thread which connects all the periods, and continues up until the present moment, is the descendants of those people who built and revered and prayed in that same Temple, and continued to mourn for it after it was destroyed — the Jewish people.

PERSIAN PERIOD (538-333 BCE)

From the books of Jeremiah (32ff) and II Kings (24-25) and from excavations, we learn that the devastation of Judah was widespread. When Gedaliah, who had been appointed governor by the Babylonians, was murdered, many of those who had not been exiled fled. The Babylonians did not bring in other people (as did the Assyrians when the kingdom of Israel was destroyed) so the population of Judah decreased and consisted of "vine-growers and husbandmen" (II Kings 25:12).

Cyrus (who is viewed by Isaiah as "the Lord's anointed") founded the Persian Empire and in 538 BCE conquered Babylon. The exiles were given permission to return to Jerusalem and rebuild their Temple (Ezra 1:2-3). The prophets Hagai and Zechariah encouraged Sheshbazzar and Zerubabel, who led the returning exiles.

Written sources for this period are scanty but c. 458 BCE Ezra called a convocation of the people at which they renewed their covenant with God. Due to the opposition of the people of Samaria, Ezra was unable to complete the walls of Jerusalem. This was accomplished by Nehemiah.

> "This is the word of the Lord... Not by might, nor by power, but by My spirit, saith the Lord of hosts."
> *Zechariah 4:6*

Praying at the Western Wall — the Kotel

Jewish cemetery on
Mount of Olives

"Jerusalem shall be inhabited as towns without walls
for the multitude of men and cattle therein."

Zechariah 2:8

"Then shall the Lord go forth, and fight against those
nations, as when He fought in the day of battle. And His
feet shall stand in that day upon the Mount of Olives,
which is before Jerusalem on the east, and the Mount of
Olives shall cleave in the midst thereof toward the east
and toward the west, and there shall be a very great
valley; and half of the mountain shall remove toward the
north, and half of it toward the south."

Zechariah 14:3-4

Papyri, found in Elephantine (Leontis) in Egypt and Wadi Dalya in the Jordan Valley, add to our very meager knowledge of this period. Coins and jug handles imprinted with "Yahud" (Judah) confirm that Judea was an autonomous province of the Persian Empire.

The population of the land was varied. Edomites lived in the Negev and as far north as Hebron; the seafaring Phoenicians lived along the northern coast; the Samaritans occupied what had been the kingdom of Israel. In Judea were the Judaeans, later to be called Jews, with pockets of Sidonians in such places as Maresha.

It is towards the end of this period that the Samaritans made their final break from Judaism. They no longer performed their religious worship or offered sacrifices at the Temple in Jerusalem. Instead they built a temple on Mount Gerizim and appointed their own high priest. They continued to use the Torah but rejected the Oral Law.

This period came to an end with the rise of Alexander of Macedon, under whose leadership the Persian Empire was conquered.

Sidonian Tomb at Maresha / Beit Guvrin; the Sidonians were mercenaries who settled in the area during the Hellenistic period

HELLENISTIC PERIOD 333-63 BCE

As we have seen, historical events in the land of Israel were intrinsically woven into the changes that took place in the Fertile Crescent and Egypt. At this point in history the seat of power shifted westwards to the Mediterranean basin, to the Greek Empire.

The army of Alexander the Great conquered Judah in 332 BCE and swept eastward as far as India. In its wake a new culture took hold — Hellenism.

The untimely death of Alexander, before he was able to consolidate his empire, resulted in its division into three sections — Greece and the Islands, Egypt (ruled by Ptolemy) and Syria (ruled by the Seleucids).

Judea, after initially being tossed between the Ptolemies and Seleucids in 301 BCE, fell to the Ptolemies and, for the next hundred years, was ruled from Egypt.

Independent administration was introduced with a localized tax system. Greek architecture and town planning led to the spread of new cities (*poleis*). Agriculture flourished and oil, balsam and asphalt were in great demand as exports. Mercenaries and colonists swelled the local population with pagan settlers and temples.

CONQUESTS OF THE HASMONEAN DYNASTY (166-76 BCE)

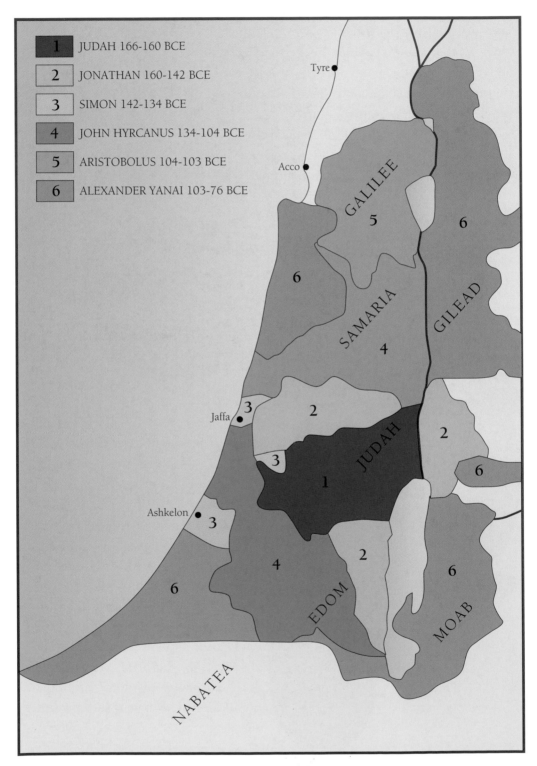

Legend:
- **1** JUDAH 166-160 BCE
- **2** JONATHAN 160-142 BCE
- **3** SIMON 142-134 BCE
- **4** JOHN HYRCANUS 134-104 BCE
- **5** ARISTOBOLUS 104-103 BCE
- **6** ALEXANDER YANAI 103-76 BCE

Tyre

Acco

GALILEE 5

6

SAMARIA 4

GILEAD

Jaffa 3

2

JUDAH

2

6

3

1

Ashkelon 3

4

2

6

EDOM

MOAB

6

NABATEA

Banias, site of the pagan temple and the source of one of the tributaries of the Jordan River

Under the Ptolemies the Jewish population enjoyed religious freedom but this came to an end in 201 BCE. At the Battle of Paneum (Banias) the Seleucids gained control of the area, now to be known as Coele-Syria and Phoenicia.

Jerusalem, although not a *polis*, continued to be capital of Judea, an autonomous area governed by the high priest and the Council of Elders.

Antiochus Epiphanes (175-164 BCE), needing the revenue provided by polis taxes and temple treasuries, decided to accelerate the Hellenization process. Jerusalem was made a polis, and named Antiochia. The usual institutions, including a gymnasium next to the Temple, were built. A new high priest was appointed, subservient to Antiochus, and not of the line of Zadok.

During an unsuccessful Seleucid invasion of Egypt, partly due to the interference of Rome, there were revolts in Judea, including in Jerusalem, against the Seleucids. The deposed high priest, Jason, was reinstated.

Antiochus retaliated by taking complete control of Jerusalem. The Temple was dedicated to Zeus and strategically overlooking the Temple, the citadel, Acra, was built.

Circumcision and Sabbath observance were banned, thereby threatening the practice of the Jewish religion. As the Jewish population was forced to participate in the pagan rites at the Temple, many Jews left Jerusalem.

Despite the fact that many of the priests in Jerusalem were Hellenists, having been appointed by Antiochus, the general population remained faithful to their religion. They rallied to the banner of Mattathias, a priest living in Modi'in, who called on the people to defy the ban against Jewish observances.

Led by Judah the Maccabee (166-160 BCE), son of Mathathias, the rebels won a number of significant battles against the Seleucid forces. In 164 BCE they regained control of Jerusalem and rededicated the Temple, even though a Seleucid force held out in the Acra.

The Jewish holiday of Hanukkah (Festival of Lights) commemorates this rededication of the Temple. The events leading up to the revolt and the early years of the Hasmonean dynasty are preserved in the books of the Maccabees.

Initially, the rebels suffered some setbacks and temporarily lost Jerusalem, but under Jonathan (160-143 BCE), brother of and successor to Judah, more areas came under Hasmonean rule.

Diplomacy and politics were as important as victory in battle. Under Judah, a treaty had been signed with Rome, thereby recognizing Judea as an independent power. Jonathan played off Demetrius I and Alexander Balas, rival aspirants, for control of the Seleucid kingdom, and so gained more territory as well as the position of high priest.

> "We kindle these lights on account of the miracles, the deliverances and the wonders which Thou didst work for our fathers, by means of Thy holy priests. During all the eight days of Hanukkah these lights are sacred, neither is it permitted us to make any profane use of them; but we are only to look at them, in order that we may give thanks unto Thy name for Thy miracles, Thy deliverances and Thy wonders."
>
> *Blessing after kindling the first light*

These intrigues eventually cost him his life as he was murdered by Tryphon, to whom he had switched his allegiance, but not before he had established relations with Sparta.

His brother Simon (143-134 BCE) continued to expand the independent areas of Judea.

> "King Alexander (Balas of the Seleucid kingdom) to his brother Jonathan, greeting. We have heard about you, that you are a mighty warrior and worthy to be our friend. And so we have appointed you today to be the high priest of your nation; you are to be called the king's friend."
>
> *I Mac 10:18-20*

HASMONEAN & HERODIAN DYNASTIES

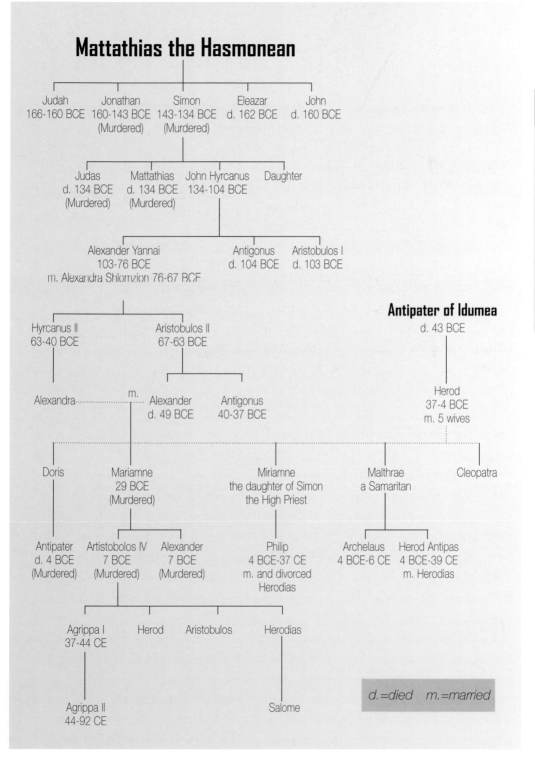

Mattathias the Hasmonean

Judah 166-160 BCE
Jonathan 160-143 BCE (Murdered)
Simon 143-134 BCE (Murdered)
Eleazar d. 162 BCE
John d. 160 BCE

Judas d. 134 BCE (Murdered)
Mattathias d. 134 BCE (Murdered)
John Hyrcanus 134-104 BCE
Daughter

Alexander Yannai 103-76 BCE
m. Alexandra Shlomzion 76-67 BCE
Antigonus d. 104 BCE
Aristobulos I d. 103 BCE

Hyrcanus II 63-40 BCE
Aristobulos II 67-63 BCE

Antipater of Idumea
d. 43 BCE

Alexandra ········ m. ····· Alexander d. 49 BCE
Antigonus 40-37 BCE

Herod 37-4 BCE m. 5 wives

Doris
Mariamne 29 BCE (Murdered)
Miriamne the daughter of Simon the High Priest
Malthrae a Samaritan
Cleopatra

Antipater d. 4 BCE (Murdered)
Artistobolos IV 7 BCE (Murdered)
Alexander 7 BCE (Murdered)
Philip 4 BCE-37 CE m. and divorced Herodias
Archelaus 4 BCE-6 CE
Herod Antipas 4 BCE-39 CE m. Herodias

Agrippa I 37-44 CE
Herod
Aristobulos
Herodias

Agrippa II 44-92 CE
Salome

d.=died   m.=married

Exemption from paying tribute to the royal treasury and the privilege of minting his own coins indicates to us the degree of independence enjoyed by the Hasmonean kingdom of Judah.

In 140 BCE the great assembly in Jerusalem conferred on Simon the titles "ethnarch, high priest and supreme commander of the Judaean nation" and declared these positions hereditary "until a true prophet shall arise" (I Mac 14:27ff).

The conquest of Jaffa and Gezer gave access to the sea and the conquest of the Acra restored Jerusalem entirely to Hasmonean rule. Simon (together with two of his sons) was assassinated by his son-in-law.

His third son, John Hyrcanus 134-104 BCE, also exploited the Seleucid-Ptolemian rivalry and expanded even further, absorbing Idumea (Edom) and areas across the Jordan. He also destroyed the Samaritan temple on Mount Gerizim.

During the rule of Alexander Yannai, 103-76 BCE, whose title was king, the territory of Judea reached its peak and included control of the Nabataeans. However, for the first time, there was conflict within the Hasmonean kingdom.

The Sadducees (Zedukim, priestly caste) served in the Temple. They had been the vanguard of the Hasmonean revolt but in the intervening years had lost their influence over the people, had become the aristocratic rich upper class and were often corrupt. It may be that this is the period when the Dead Sea sects, including the Essenes, first came into being.

The Pharisees (Perushim, those who leave or those who interpret) were the sages, the proponents of the Oral Law. The people respected them and their leadership.

Alexander's support of the Sadducees resulted in a revolt of the Pharisees which was cruelly suppressed. Too late he understood his misjudgment and on his deathbed he urged his wife, Shlomzion Alexandra (76-67 BCE), to compromise with the Pharisees.

During her peaceful rule the Pharisees increased their influence.

Upon her death, her son Aristobulus II (67-63 BCE) ousted his older brother, Hyrcanus II (63-40 BCE), thereby hastening the end of the rule of the Hasmonean dynasty.

Hyrcanus was assisted by Antipater the Idumean and Aretas the Nabataean. At first, Rome intervened in favor of Aristobulus. Pompey conquered Syria, made it a Roman province and then switched his support to Hyrcanus.

Judea was confined to the areas of Judah, southern Samaria, the Galilee and those parts on the other side of the Jordan with a large Jewish population (Peraea) and had to pay tribute to Rome. Hyrcanus was reduced from king to ethnarch but remained high priest.

And so the Roman period is ushered in.

ROMAN PERIOD 63 BCE - 633 CE
GENERAL INTRODUCTION

This period can be subdivided into three periods:

The first is 63 BCE to 70 CE. The Second Temple was under Jewish control and at times Rome allowed the transfer of a Temple tax paid by Jews throughout the Empire to be transferred to Jerusalem. The population of Judea, Galilee and neighboring areas enjoyed a fluctuating amount of autonomy, ranging from an independent vassal kingdom to direct rule by Roman governors. The Roman Empire was pagan.

The second period is from 70 CE to 333 CE. Rome continued to be pagan. With the destruction of the Temple and the conquest of Galilee and Judea, the Jews lost most of their independence. During this period the Mishnah and Jerusalem Talmud (Oral Law) were redacted.

The final period is from 333 CE to 633 CE. Christianity became the official religion in what remained of the Roman Empire, part of which had been conquered by the Visigoths, Vandals and barbarians. The Holy Land is ruled by the eastern Byzantine Empire. During this period the Babylonian Talmud was redacted.

Left: Roman statue in the Sdot-Yam Museum of Caesarea Antiquities
Below: One of the mosaic floors in Sepphoris (Zippori) depicting scenes from the life of Dionysus, the mythical god of wine

ROMAN PERIOD (63 BCE - 70 CE)

As we saw in the last chapter, with the ascent of Pompey in Rome and the Roman takeover of Judea, the size of Judea was reduced as was the status of Hyrcanus. However, both Hyrcanus and Antipater joined Julius Caesar's camp and when Caesar defeated Pompey in 48 BCE, Caesar was generous to both.

Aerial view of Herodium in the Judean desert

Hyrcanus was reinstated as hereditary ethnarch and Antipater's son, Herod, was appointed governor of Galilee.

Caesar's assassination (44 BCE) did not cause any major upheaval in Judea until the Parthian invasion (40 BCE). Antigonus, son of Hyrcanus's brother and ex-rival, Aristobulus, allied with the Parthians in an attempt to regain the throne, which he considered to be rightly his.

With the people's support Hyrcanus was imprisoned and his ally, Herod the Idumean, was forced to flee to Rome to seek military aid. Antigonus was crowned King of Judea by the people.

In Rome, Anthony and Octavian concluded that Herod was the only one they could trust in Judea and bestowed on him the title of king. The Roman army succeeded in turning the tide and the Parthians were pushed back, leaving Antigonus without military support.

Herod returned to Judea and with Roman assistance gained control of Idumea, Samaria and the Galilee. When the Parthians were finally defeated, the Roman legions were available to enable Herod to take all of Judea, including Jerusalem. In 37 BCE Antigonus was executed, thereby ending the Hasmonean dynasty.

Herod was completely loyal to Rome, first to Anthony, who had presented the area of Jericho and the lucrative balsam groves to Cleopatra, and then to Augustus. His subjugation of the Nabataeans proved his value to the Romans and the area under his control was increased to include Gaulanitis, Batanaea and Trachonitis in the northeast.

The Nabateans were probably nomadic tribes who had migrated from the Arabian peninsula. They settled in the area known as Idumea (Edom) and their capital was at Petra, excavated in Jordan. Familiar with desert life, they controlled the spice trade from the east. Along the desert route they maintained settlements which offered a resting place with fresh food and water. Some of these sites have been excavated in the south of Israel. They had supported the Parthians in their wars with Rome.

Opposite page: Remains from Nabataean towns in the Negev

While the Jews of the diaspora benefited from Herod's personal relations with the Roman aristocracy from Augustus down, his own subjects did not. Only the fear that a revolt would diminish his prestige in the eyes of the Romans limited his cruelty, oppression and even heavier taxation.

Key administrative posts were given to non-Jews or Hellenist Jews. He appointed as high priest only those who would serve him faithfully, often from the Hellenist diaspora. The priests were subservient to the high priest, so politics, and not religion, became the guiding light of many of them, leading to the corruption to which both Jesus and Josephus Flavius refer.

Herod built the port and city of Caesarea, through which silks and spices from the Far East were shipped to the Roman Empire. Control of this trade generated the revenue to finance the building of palaces and fortresses throughout the country, many of which have since been exposed by archaeological excavations.

Opposite page: Entrance to complex of tombs excavated near the King David Hotel and thought to be the Herodian family tombs
Left: Roman sculpture and coin in the Sdot-Yam Museum of Caesarea Antiquities
Below: Aqueduct at Caesarea

The pride of Herod's accomplishments — the extension of, and the buildings on, the Temple Mount, including further enhancement of the Temple itself — were destroyed by the Romans in the year 70 CE, as was all that he built in Jerusalem. Only the Western Wall (the Kotel) remains.

Herod married five times. Antipater, his son by his first wife, he executed shortly before he died. He also murdered his second wife, Miriamne, granddaughter of Hyrcanus II, and their two sons Aristobulus IV and Alexander. His third wife was Miriamne, daughter of Simon the High Priest.

With Herod's death in 4 BCE his kingdom was divided between his sons. Archelaus inherited Judea, Idumea and Samaria. His brother Herod Antipas inherited the Galilee and the Peraea (Jewish Transjordan) and their half-brother Philip inherited the Golan and the northeast part of the kingdom.

About this time Joseph and Mary left Nazareth where they lived, to go to Bethlehem because of a census which the Romans had ordered (Luke 2:1-4). There Jesus was born.

Roman theater at Caesarea

DIVISION OF HEROD'S KINGDOM (4BCE)

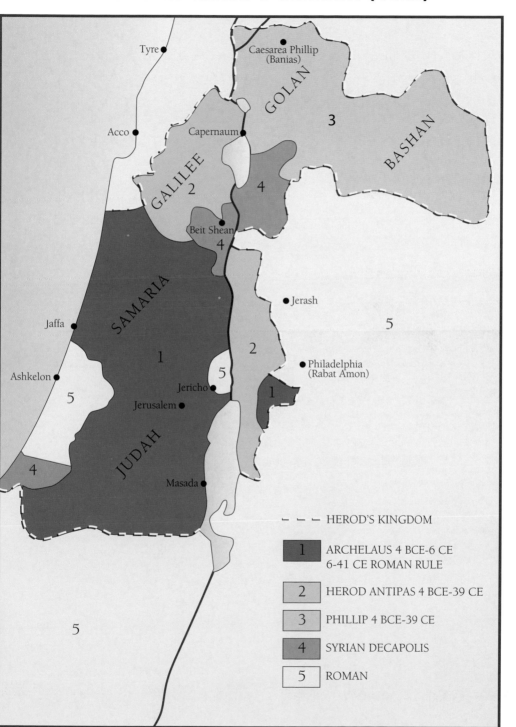

Tyre

Caesarea Phillip
(Banias)

GOLAN

3

BASHAN

Acco

Capernaum

GALILEE

2

4

Beit Shean

4

SAMARIA

Jerash

5

Jaffa

1

2

Philadelphia
(Rabat Amon)

Ashkelon

5

Jericho

5

1

Jerusalem

JUDAH

Masada

- - - HEROD'S KINGDOM

1	ARCHELAUS 4 BCE-6 CE 6-41 CE ROMAN RULE
2	HEROD ANTIPAS 4 BCE-39 CE
3	PHILLIP 4 BCE-39 CE
4	SYRIAN DECAPOLIS
5	ROMAN

The Roman Jewish historian Josephus Flavius tells us that when Archelaus was deposed by Rome in 6 CE and his domain became a Roman province known as Judea, the Roman governor Quirinius conducted a census.

The capital was moved from Jerusalem to Caesarea where the prefect and later procurator resided. Judea was no more than a satellite of the province of Syria where the bulk of the Roman army was stationed.

The Sanhedrin in Jerusalem continued to serve as the highest authority in matters of religion but no longer had the right to try capital cases, as is borne out by John (18:31).

Opposite page: Monumental burial tombs in the Kidron Valley
Left: Bell tower of the Church of the Nativity
Below: The Church of the Annunciation in Nazareth

Synagogue at Capernaum

Dissatisfaction with Roman rule increased during the procuratorship of Pontius Pilate (26-36 CE), who deliberately refused to show tolerance for Jewish religious susceptibilities. He minted coins with pagan cultic symbols and plundered the Temple treasury. There were numerous clashes between the Jewish population and the Roman legionnaires including one such clash mentioned by Luke (13:1).

Herod Antipas ruled Galilee and Peraea. In Galilee he founded the city of Tiberias, which he named in honor of his patron Tiberius. Generally he was sensitive to the requirements of his Jewish population. However, it was he who, at the request of his step-daughter Salome, executed John the Baptist who preached against his marriage to Herodias, the ex-wife of his half-brother Philip.

All that we know of Jesus and his ministry comes to us from the New Testament which was canonized in the second half of the fourth century. Made up of twenty-seven books, these do not appear in the order in which they were written.

Of the three Synoptic Gospels (gospel = *evangelium* = good news), it was thought that Mark was the earliest, written in the third quarter of the first century (over forty years after the crucifixion), and that Matthew and Luke appeared to have used Mark as a source. However, there is a new school of thought which holds that perhaps Luke is the earlier source. John was written in the last decade of the first century and may have used Mark and Luke but is more theological than the Synoptic Gospels.

Luke is presumed to have also written the Book of Acts, which deals mainly with the lives of Peter and Paul. John is presumed to have also written the Book of Revelation, which is an eschatological prophecy. The remaining twenty-one books are letters, about half of them written by Paul, describing the early church and its developing theology.

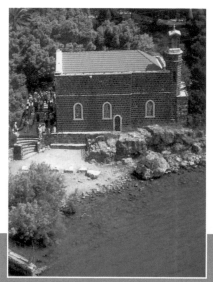

Until the end of the nineteenth century the King James Bible was the best-known English translation. It was based on the Latin Vulgate and the Greek Septuagint manuscripts. With the discovery of even earlier manuscripts, contemporary new translations have corrected errors in the first translations and modernized the language.

Left: The Primacy of St. Peter on the Sea of Galilee
Below: Modern wooden boats, modeled after
the two-thousand-year-old boat excavated from
the mud on the receding shores of the Sea of Galilee

Although the gospels do not give dates for the ministry of Jesus, it is usually placed between the years 28 and 30 CE. Most of the disciples of Jesus were fishermen on the Kinneret (the Sea of Galilee). He grew up, preached and performed most of His miracles in Galilee where the sites were hallowed by His followers.

Judea was governed by Pontius Pilate, so, when visiting Jerusalem, as a Galilean, Jesus was technically in a foreign country. At the time of Jesus' trial, Herod Antipas was visiting Jerusalem, which was not within his jurisdiction, even though Jesus was one of his subjects.

The authority of the high priest and the Sanhedrin was limited to matters relating to religious laws. The authority of Pontius Pilate was paramount. Crucifixion was a punishment used frequently by the Romans.

Procession near the Jordan River celebrating the baptism of Jesus

Understanding the historical background of the period and visiting the places mentioned can give a new dimension and deeper understanding of the gospels.

Philip died in 34 CE and the area he ruled was incorporated into the province of Syria. In 37 CE it was assigned by Caligula, the new emperor, to his friend Agrippa I, grandson of Herod and Mariamne, son of the murdered Aristobulus IV. Agrippa I was proclaimed king, and in 39 CE he received the domain of Herod Antipas, who was exiled to Gaul.

Above: Podium of a statue or back rest of a seat? Found at the Roman theater at Caesarea and showing the letters "...ius Pilatus"
Left: On a specially minted coin the Romans announced to the world, "Judea Capta," Judea has been captured, the Jewish revolt is over

Agrippa was an able statesman and succeeded in dissuading Caligula from his plan to place a golden statue of himself in the Temple in Jerusalem. He was also instrumental in assuring the Senate's support for Claudius, who was proclaimed emperor by the army after the assassination of Caligula.

As a token of gratitude Judea and Samaria were added to his kingdom which now encompassed all the areas ruled by his grandfather, Herod. With his death in 44, his son Agrippa II continued as king but Judea reverted to Roman rule under a procurator. Throughout the rule of Nero (54-68), Rome was in turmoil and each procurator was worse than his predecessor. The people were oppressed and over-taxed.

Josephus Flavius described the division in the Jewish population. There were the followers of the aristocratic Sadducees, the priestly caste, who were dependent on the Romans for their positions. The Pharisees and their followers were interested in safeguarding Jewish religious belief and practice and their attitude to Rome was moderate.

Virulently anti-Roman were the various zealot groups, whose aim was to expel the Romans and gain complete independence. They were able to gain support by promising the masses social reforms.

Last, but not least, there were the Essenes, about whom we learn from the Dead Sea Scrolls. They had separated themselves from both the Sadducees and the Pharisees, believing that Judaism and the Temple had become corrupt. "Sons of Light" is how they defined themselves. They used the solar calendar (introduced during the time of Julius Caesar in 46 BCE) and celebrated the festivals on a different date from the main body of Jews, who continued using the lunar calendar.

(The lunar calendar is shorter than the solar by eleven days. To ensure that the festivals are celebrated in the correct season an extra month is added to the Hebrew calendar seven times in every cycle of nineteen years).

Unrest was widespread and a general revolt was a matter of time. The immediate cause was a series of events that began when Jews and pagans clashed in Caesarea. Rioting spread to Jerusalem. Agrippa II tried to restore order but the riots spread throughout the province.

The Romans assembled a large force and marched against Jerusalem but were repulsed by the fury of the crowds. This limited victory encouraged more people to follow the banner of the revolt.

Nero sent Vespasian with an army of sixty thousand to quell the revolt. Galilee was subdued, including the fortress at Jotpata. The commander of Jotpata, Joseph ben Mattathias, surrendered to Vespasian and eventually became a Roman citizen and court historian, known to us as Josephus Flavius.

Much of what we know about the great revolt, as well as about the history of the Jewish people from the Hasmonean revolt up to his times, is preserved in the books he wrote.

Excavated remains of a house in the upper part of the city, destroyed in 70 CE

Above: Aerial view of Masada
Left: Synagogue of Masada

In a short time the Romans completed the conquest of Judea but the upheaval in Rome, due to Nero's death in 68 CE, delayed the final blow to Jerusalem.

Vespasian was recalled to Rome and declared emperor. When he had restored law and order he sent his son Titus to complete the campaign against Jerusalem.

The various factions in Jerusalem had not utilized the interlude to formulate a joint defense plan. Titus attacked from the north, breached the third and then the second walls, besieged the Antonia fortress, razed it and, on the ninth day of the month of Av the Temple was taken and immediately

Opposite page: On the ninth day of the month of Av
Jews gather at the Western Wall (the Kotel) and remember the destruction of the First and Second Temples

destroyed. Within a short time the rest of the city fell. So thorough was the Roman destruction of Jerusalem that it burned for days — proof of which can today be seen in excavations.

The last places still holding out were Machaerus, on the eastern shore of the Dead Sea, and Masada, on the western side. According to Josephus, the people of Machaerus were tricked into surrendering.

The defenders of Masada, lead by Yair ben Eleazar, decided after a three-year siege to "die unenslaved" by their enemies. When the Romans completed their final assault they were confronted with rows of dead bodies. They "did not exult over them as enemies but admired the nobility of their resolve" (Josephus Flavius, *The Jewish War*).

These events bring to a close the Second Temple period and with it the end of Jewish autonomy. During the next two millennia Jews will mourn the destruction of the Temple and pray to be able to return to Jerusalem. Those who do will pray at the Kotel, the Western Wall, also known as the Wailing Wall.

> "Rejoice ye with Jerusalem, and be glad with her, all ye that love her: rejoice for joy with her, all ye that mourn for her."
>
> Isaiah 66:10
> Inscription on the stone
> under Robinson's Arch

The southern corner of the Western Wall of the Temple Mount, showing the protruding stones of Robinson's Arch. Along the exposed pavement is the evidence of the destruction, by the Romans in 70 CE, of the buildings which stood on the Temple Mount

"Of their forts the fifty strongest were razed to the ground. Nine hundred and eighty-five of their best-known villages were destroyed.... Thus the whole of Judah became a desert, as indeed had been foretold to the Jews before the war...and wolves and hyenas, many in number, roamed howling through their cities."

Dio Cassius,
History of the Romans
describing the aftermath
of the Bar Kochba revolt

CHAPTER 6

70-633   Mishnah and Talmud

Although historically we remain in the Roman-pagan period, we are using a new chapter heading, for this is the period in which the Oral Law, companion to the biblical laws of the Torah, was codified.

As thorough as the Roman destruction was, by the beginning of the second century there appears to have been a substantial recovery. Towns and villages were rebuilt and agriculture revived. The only thing never to grow again in the land of Israel were the persimmons of Ein Gedi, destroyed together with the secret of producing their famous balsam.

With the loss of the Temple there was a feeling of despair as to the future of Jewish traditional life which was so dependent on the Temple and its rituals. To Rabbi Yohanan ben Zakkai goes the credit for reestablishing Jewish communal life.

Opposite page: Olive oil storage room in the Hazan caves, from the time of the revolt against the Romans, 132 CE

Below: View of Tiberias from the Tomb of Rabbi Meir Baal HaNes

Above: Peki'in Synagogue
Right: Bar'am Synagogue

Deputy head of the Sanhedrin, he had escaped from Jerusalem in 70 CE. He was detained by the Romans at Yavneh (one of the places to which those who had surrendered to the Romans were taken) and there he revived the Sanhedrin and opened an academy. From there he proclaimed the sighting of the new moon, an important element in setting the dates of festivals, as the Jewish calendar is lunar.

The synagogue (Beit Knesset — house of gathering), which until this time was where people gathered to learn the Torah (Law), now became a place of prayer as well, incorporating some of the liturgy of the Temple. To recall the sacrifice of oil in the menorah (seven-branched candelabra), Jews would light Sabbath candles. To recall the sacrifice of wheat and the loaves on the shrew-bread table they would use a special plaited loaf (hallah) for their Sabbath meal.

Following in his wake, eminent sages and rabbis set up their houses of study throughout the country. It was in the Beit Midrash (academy) of Rabbi Akiva in Bnei Brak that the Passover Haggadah was finalized. In a sense this replaced the sacrificial and pilgrimage rituals of Pesach celebration in the time of the Temple.

I t is told that when Rabbi Akiva and his companions, Rabbis Gamliel, Eleazar and Joshua saw a fox run through the ruins of the Temple, they wept and he alone laughed. To his surprised companions he explained: "The prophecy 'Therefore shall Zion for your sake be plowed as a field, and Jerusalem shall become heaps, and the mountain of the house as the high places of the forest' (Micah 3:12) is recorded and fulfilled. Surely then the prophecy 'There shall yet old men and old women dwell in the streets of Jerusalem...and the streets of the city shall be full of boys and girls playing in the streets thereof' (Zech 8:4-5) which is recorded, shall be fulfilled."

During the rule of Trajan there was a Jewish revolt in Mesopotamia, 115-117 CE, ruthlessly suppressed by Lucius Quietus. This foreshadowed events to come. A decade later, during a visit to the east, Hadrian decided to make Jerusalem a pagan city and among other restrictions forbade circumcision.

A revolt led by Bar Kochba, with the support of Rabbi Akiva, broke out. The little we know of this revolt comes mainly from the Roman historian Dio Cassius and from archaeological excavations. Galilee was

Right: Headless statue of Hadrian, found in the excavated Cardo of Caesarea
Below: Entrance to the catacombs at Beit Shearim, burial place of Judah HaNasi and one of the seats of the Sanhedrin

subdued earlier on, but in Judea, coins minted in "year four of the redemption of Israel" were found.

The last fortress to fall, in 135 CE, was Betar. The revolt, coming a mere sixty-two years after the great revolt, was so intense that the Romans had to send reinforcements from all over the empire. Their losses were so great that Dio Cassius wrote that Hadrian, in his dispatch to the Senate, refrained from using the customary introduction "I and my troops are well."

Judea lay wasted, its population sold into slavery. The Romans built a new city on the ruins of Jerusalem, naming it Aelia Capitolina, after the emperor Aelius Adrianus, but this new name did not stick. The name of the province was also changed, from Judea to Syria-Palestina, an appellation in use, in one form or another, until the establishment of the State of Israel in 1948.

An entire generation of sages perished in the Roman persecutions that followed, including Rabbi Shimon Bar Yochai, in whose memory the festival of Lag B'Omer is celebrated.

The Sanhedrin moved to Galilee, first to Usha then to Beit Shearim (c. 170), to Sepphoris (c. 200) and finally to Tiberias (c. 235). With the rise to power of the Severan dynasty in Rome, the persecution of Jews diminished.

Rabbi Judah HaNasi (the Prince), who led the Sanhedrin, was instrumental in the redaction of the Mishnah (c. 200).

The Mishnah is divided into six orders which are in turn divided into tractates. The Oral Law (*halachah* — pl. *halachot*), which explains and expounds

Burial ground near Mishmar HaEmek

Left: A page of the Talmud. The first two and a half lines of the central panel are the Mishnah. The continuation is the Gemara. The framing columns are later commentaries.

TRANSLATION AND COMMENTARY

[76A] ¹On the other hand, **if the employer retracts and dismisses the workers** after they have begun the work for which they have been hired, **he is at a disadvantage.** Accordingly, if wages have risen since the workers were first hired, the employer must pay them as agreed for the part of the work they have done. If, however, wages have fallen, he must pay the workers the full amount he originally promised them, less whatever he will now have to pay new workers to complete the task. ²The Mishnah concludes with two general rules: ³Whoever deviates from the terms of an agreement between an employer and a worker **is at a disadvantage.** For example, if someone brings wool to a dyer to be dyed red and the dyer dyes it black, the dyer is not entitled to his full wages because he deviated from the agreement between the two parties. In such a case, the dyer is entitled either to the expenses he incurred in dyeing the wool black or to the value he added to the wool, whichever is less. ⁴Likewise, **whoever retracts** — this expression is explained by the Gemara below, 77b — **is at a disadvantage.**

GEMARA חֲזַר זֶה בּוֹ וְזֶה בּוֹ לֹא קָתָנֵי ¹The Gemara begins its discussion with an analysis of the first clause of the Mishnah, which stated that if workers are hired and one party misleads the other, the misled party has grounds for resentment against the other party but cannot press a monetary claim against him. The Gemara first wishes to determine the nature of the deception referred to in the Mishnah. It notes that the **Mishnah does not state** "**one or the other retracted**," which we would have understood as referring to a situation where the employer dismissed the workers or the workers refused to work, ²but rather the Mishnah states that "**they misled each other.**" Since the Mishnah does not speak of the parties *retracting,* but of *misleading* each other, it must be referring to a case where one party misled the other about the terms of employment. Now, assuming that the Mishnah is dealing with deception rather than retraction, the case is not one where the employer misled the workers or vice versa, but rather where the **workers themselves misled each other,** presumably by misrepresenting among themselves the terms of employment offered by the employer.

LITERAL TRANSLATION

[76A] ¹If the employer (lit., "the householder") retracts, he is at a disadvantage. ²Whoever deviates is at a disadvantage. ³and whoever retracts is at a disadvantage.

GEMARA ⁴[The Mishnah] does not state "And one or the other retracted," ⁵but "And they misled each other," [implying] that the workers misled each other

RASHI

ואם בעל הבית חוזר – וכו׳ ...

NOTES

חָזַר זֶה בּוֹ וְזֶה בּוֹ לֹא קָתָנֵי אֶלָּא, וְהִטְעוּ זֶה אֶת זֶה, דְּאַטְעוּ פּוֹעֲלִים אַהֲדָדֵי **The Mishnah does not state: "And one or the other retracted," but: "And they misled each other."** The Gemara assumes that the Mishnah is referring to a case where one of the workers misled the others, because it seems to have had difficulty in constructing a case where the workers or the employer misled each other. The Jerusalem Talmud, however, interprets the Mishnah as referring to a case where the workers misled the employer or vice versa when negotiating the terms of employment. The worker that the employer told the worker that most workers earn ten zuz a day when in fact they are paid only five, or the employer told the workers that the standard pay is five zuz a day when in fact most workers earn ten. According to the Jerusalem Talmud, the Mishnah rules that in either case the agreement is binding and the party misled has grounds for resentment only. Indeed, *Ra'avad* asks why our Gemara did not explain the Mishnah the same way as did the Jerusalem Talmud since ...

וְאִם בַּעַל הַבַּיִת חוֹזֵר **If the employer retracts.** Our commentary follows *Rashi,* who explains that the employer is always at a disadvantage, regardless of whether labor costs increase or decrease. Specifically, if wages rise, the employer must pay the workers for the work they have done according to the rate that was originally promised them, even though it will now cost him more to finish the work. And if wages fall, the employer must pay the workers what he originally stipulated, minus whatever is necessary to complete the work.

Other commentators, however, maintain that the employer is only "at a disadvantage" if wages rise (as explained above), but if wages fall, he need pay them only for the work they have done at the rate promised — for if he were required to pay the workers their full salary minus the cost of completing the work, he would then end up paying them more than the actual value of their work (*Talmud Rabbeinu Peretz* in the name of *Ri*).

Right: The English translation relates only to the first five lines of the photograph above.

the biblical commandments, and traditionally was given to Moses together with the Torah, is derived from the biblical commandments, evolved over the centuries. The discussions and controversies of its formative period are preserved in the Mishnah.

Halachot not included in the Mishnah are known as the Tosefta and still later discussions are the Gemara. The Mishnah, Tosefta and Gemara together form the basis for the Talmud.

The Jerusalem Talmud was finally redacted c. 350 and is a commentary on, and an elaboration, clarification and updating of the Mishnah. It concentrates on those *halachot* (laws) relevant to life in the Holy Land.

The Babylonian Talmud, a parallel development in the diaspora (Jewish dispersion), emphasizes those *halachot* relevant to life in exile from the Holy Land. It was redacted about a century later.

The Hebrew calendar is lunar and consists of 354 days, making it eleven days shorter than the solar calendar. The festivals, which originate in the Torah, are related to the seasons. One month before Passover the sages went into the fields to see if the barley would ripen in time for the Passover festival. If not, they would announce a second month of Adar (which falls in February). Based on astronomical research and records kept over many centuries the calendar was fixed in 358 CE. Over a period of nineteen years seven leap year months are added. This was dispatched to Jewish communities throughout the diaspora and is still in use today.

The signs of the Zodiac on the mosaic floor of the synagogue at Beit Alpha; these astrological symbols follow the lunar, not solar, months

Beit Shean
archaeological site

(Muslims, who also use the lunar calendar, do not intercalate, so the Muslim year is eleven and a quarter days shorter than the solar year used by most of the world.)

Despite attempts to prevent Jews from referring to the Talmud — and even public burnings of the Talmud — it will continue to serve as a guide to Jews all over the world in their day-to-day lives. It records the sayings and rulings of the Sages but is, at the same time, one of the most comprehensive legal codices in the world, and is studied not only by orthodox Jews.

A revised Hebrew edition updates the Talmud with the addition of commmentaries and footnotes which explain the Aramaic and sometimes archaic Hebrew. An English translation makes the Talmud available even to those who know no Hebrew or Aramaic. However, as with the Hebrew Scriptures, much is lost in the translation.

Byzantine Period (333-633)

The Church of the Pater Noster on the Mount of Olives where the Lord's prayer is displayed in over seventy languages

In 313 CE Constantine recognized the Christian religion and at the end of his reign declared it to be one of the official religions of the Roman Empire. Monotheism slowly replaced paganism in the Western world.

Queen Helena, mother of Constantine, visited the Holy Land and ordered the building of churches on the sites of events recorded by the Gospels. The first were in Bethlehem, birthplace of Jesus, and in Jerusalem, site of His crucifixion, burial and ascension.

Churches were also built in Galilee and Judea to commemorate the miracles performed there. In Jerusalem the churches follow Jesus' footsteps during his last days and hours. The forty Pentecostal days too, are recalled.

The dome of the Church of the Holy Sepulcher, site of the Crucifixion and Tomb

Above: The facade of the Church of the Agony in the Garden of Gethsemane
Left: Grotto of Gethsemane

Almost all of these churches will be destroyed by the Persian and Muslim conquerors. Some will be rebuilt by the Crusaders and again destroyed by the Muslim conquerors. Many will become the venue of pilgrims in the nineteenth and twentieth centuries, when modern churches are built.

In 350 CE, while Rome and Persia were at war, Gallus was appointed governor of the eastern provinces. His oppression of the Jewish population in Palestine resulted in a short revolt, centered in the towns of Zippori (Sepphoris), Tiberias and Beit Shearim, which all suffered when the revolt was quelled.

During the reign of Julian the advance of Christianity was temporarily halted and the Jews were promised that they could rebuild their Temple on the Temple Mount, which stood desolate since the destruction in 70 CE. But this was not to be. Julian was killed advancing on Persia through the Fertile Crescent in 363 CE.

The Byzantine church at Kursi on the eastern
shore of the Sea of Galilee

The ecumenical conferences at Nicaea
in 325, at Constantinople in 381, at
Ephesus in 431 and at Chalcedon in 451
shape the development of Christianity. As the
result of theological differences the Nestoreans
separate from the main body of Christianity in
431 and the Armenians, Copts, Chaldeans
and Ethiopians in 451.

Upheavals in the Roman Empire resulted in a split between the western and
eastern parts. (The second conference at
Nicaea in 787 will finalize the split between
the Eastern and Western Churches. The
center of the Byzantine [Greek] Orthodox
Church will be Constantinople and that of the
Catholic Church will be Rome.)

Mount Beatitudes above the shores of the Sea of Galilee

Throughout the eastern Byzantine Empire the position of the Jews deteriorated due to discriminatory laws. In Palestine they lost autonomous control of their religious affairs and were forbidden to proclaim the advent of the new moon.

The nineteen-year cycle of the Hebrew calendar, finalized in 358 CE and sent to Jewish communities throughout the diaspora, is still used today by Jews throughout the world.

Among those who visit the Holy Land, and leave us with tantalizing descriptions, are the anonymous pilgrim from Bordeaux in 333 CE and the nun Egeria in 381-84 CE. Eusebius wrote the Onamasticon, an invaluable list of towns and place names. St. Jerome, who lived in Bethlehem at the end of the fourth century, translated the Scriptures into Latin. Known as the Vulgate, this became the basis for the early translations into English.

Palaestina thrived. From archaeological excavations we know that there was a large Jewish population living side by side with Christians — as seen by synagogues and churches. Agriculture flourished. Its by-products, such as oil, wine, linen, etc., were highly thought of in Western markets.

Administratively Palestine was divided into Palaestina Prima, which included the Negev Desert, Judah (the areas around Jerusalem), the coastal plain and Samaria (Shomron), and Palaestina Secunda, which included the Galilee and the Decapolis, partly on the eastern bank of the Jordan River.

The Byzantine monastery of St. George in Wadi Kelt, built into the mountainside of the Judaean Hills by sixth century hermits

Under Roman law, the Samaritans (who follow the laws of the Torah but not the Oral Law) were not recognized as a separate religion, as were the Jews, and in 484 CE and 529 CE revolted against Roman oppression. Both revolts were quelled mercilessly and resulted in the decline of the Samaritans who are today a small community centered around the city of Nablus (Shechem) where they still offer sacrificial lambs at Passover.

In the sixth century, when the Roman Empire was invaded by the Visigoths, Huns and Vandals, Christian ascetics made their way to the Holy Land. Some lived in isolation in caves, others lived in small groups and yet others in monasteries. Most were in the Judaean Desert. The oldest intact monastery is St. Catherine's in Sinai which has an unexplored library of centuries-old unique manuscripts.

During the reign of Justinian there was a flurry of building in the Holy Land and many churches were enlarged, including the Church of the Nativity in Bethlehem. The Nea Church was built at the southern end of the Cardo in Jerusalem. As it was built on a platform supported on arches, it did not survive, but an inscription left by the builders was discovered in an excavation of its foundations.

A large mosaic on the floor of a monastery at Medba depicts a pilgrim map of the Holy Land at this time. The centerpiece is Jerusalem, clearly showing the Cardo and the northern gate (which have been excavated), the Church of the Holy Sepulcher and the Nea Church.

In 614 CE the Persians set out to conquer the disintegrating Byzantine Empire and the Jews joined them, hoping to throw off Christian oppression. The Persians captured Jerusalem and destroyed many churches through the land. In

629 CE the tables were turned and Heraclius restored the relics of the true cross to its rightful place in the Church of the Holy Sepulcher, but not for long.

Events in the Arabian Desert are going to bring changes to the Christian world, which at this point in history stretched from the Fertile Crescent through Asia Minor and Egypt to Europe.

Left: Cardo Maximus, the main road of Byzantine Jerusalem
Below: Part of the pilgrim map found on the floor of the monastery at Medba in Jordan; in the center is Jerusalem

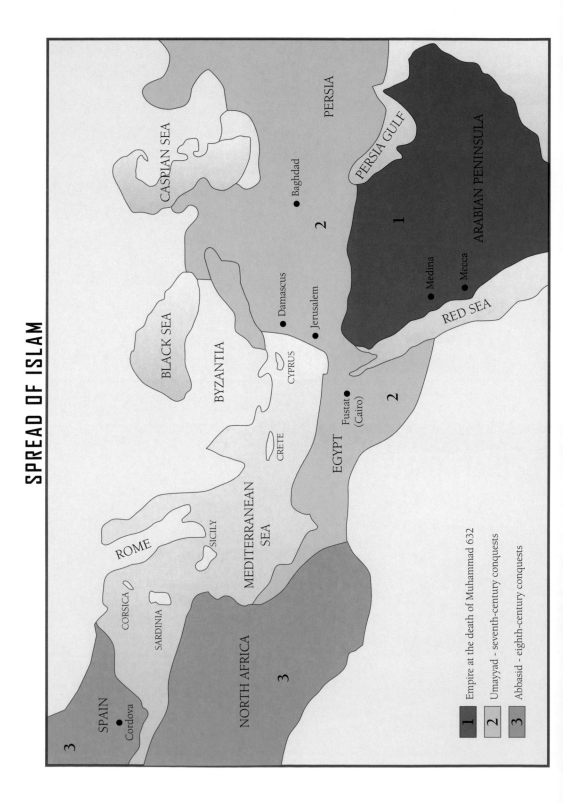

SPREAD OF ISLAM

PERSIA

PERSIA GULF

ARABIAN PENINSULA

CASPIAN SEA

● Baghdad

2

1

● Medina

● Mecca

RED SEA

BLACK SEA

● Damascus

BYZANTIA

● Jerusalem

CYPRUS

Fustat ●
(Cairo)

2

EGYPT

CRETE

ROME

SICILY

MEDITERRANEAN
SEA

CORSICA

SARDINIA

NORTH AFRICA

3

SPAIN

● Cordova

3

1 Empire at the death of Muhammad 632

2 Umayyad - seventh-century conquests

3 Abbasid - eighth-century conquests

CHAPTER 7

633-1099 Early Arab

Written sources relating to the Holy Land in this period are scant and we have to rely on historical events taking place elsewhere.

After the Persian conquest in 614 CE, Emperor Heraclius restored the Christian holy sites to Christian rule for a very short period. However the threat was no longer Persia. A new monotheistic religion had begun in the Arabian peninsula, birthplace of Muhammad.

Starting with the Arabs of the Hejaz, mainly Bedouin, by 634 CE Islam had swept through a large part of the Christian Byzantine world — the Fertile Crescent (Syria, Babylon), the Holy Land, Asia Minor (Turkey), Egypt and on to North Africa and even Spain. The dwindling Christian and Jewish population was replaced by Arab settlers from the Arabian peninsula. Christianity was replaced by Islam. Greek, the lingua franca of the entire area, was replaced by Arabic. The Bible was replaced by the Koran (Qur'an).

The Koran

The Koran (reading) was revealed to Muhammad by Allah. These revelations,

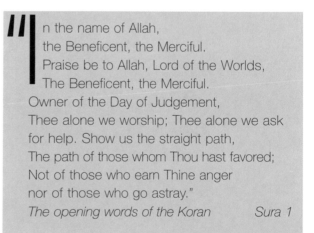

"In the name of Allah,
the Beneficent, the Merciful.
Praise be to Allah, Lord of the Worlds,
The Beneficent, the Merciful.
Owner of the Day of Judgement,
Thee alone we worship; Thee alone we ask
for help. Show us the straight path,
The path of those whom Thou hast favored;
Not of those who earn Thine anger
nor of those who go astray."
The opening words of the Koran   *Sura 1*

made during the Prophet's life in Mecca and Medina, were canonized in the time of the Caliph Othman, c. 651.

The Koran is made up of 114 *sura* (chapters). The sura are not arranged chronologically but according to length. The longest, sura 2, has 286 verses. The shortest, sura 114, has four verses.

Illuminated opening pages of the Koran

A tenth-or eleventh-century commentary added details as to where, when, and under what circumstance each sura was first spoken. The subject, whether it was said in Mecca or Medina and the number of verses appear at the beginning of each sura.

Many of the sura are influenced by both the Hebrew and Christian Scriptures. In sura 46:12 we are told: "When before it there was the Scripture of Moses, an example and a mercy; and this is a confirming Scripture in the Arabic language."

The Koran has not been as widely translated as the Bible because of the belief that the contents cannot be accurately expressed in any language other than Arabic.

Sura 1 is the prayer which devout Muslims say five times a day, usually repeated between five and seven times, accompanied by kneeling and prostrating. This is always said in Arabic.

Only on Friday, at the second prayer of the day, are Muslims obliged to go to a mosque. The prayer (rak'a) is repeated twelve times and a sermon (hutba) is given on religious or topical subjects.

The Five Pillars of Islam

1. Shahada - profession of faith
2. Salat - prayer
3. Zakat - alms to poor
4. Sawm - Ramadan fast
5. Hajj - pilgrimage to Mecca

Some Muslims add to these central tenets of the Muslim faith a sixth:
6. Jihad - personal struggle, holy war

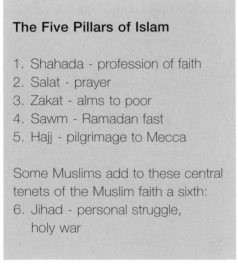

Sura 4:171 from
an English translation of
"The Holy Qur'an"
by Abdullah Yusuf Ali

The Muslim World

With the sudden death of Muhammad in 632 CE, two groups contest for the leadership, which includes secular matters such as control of the army and empire, as well as religious matters. One group, led by Abu Bakr, followed the way (sunna) of Muhammad. The other, led by Muhammad's nephew and son-in-law, Ali, believed that the leadership should come from the "tent of the prophet," his direct descendants.

Both Ali and his son, Muhammad's grandson Hussein, were murdered. Their followers decide to become a separate group (shi'a) whose spiritual leader, Imam, will always be a descendant of Muhammad.

About 90 percent of the world's Muslims are Sunni including those in the Holy Land. The Druze, Alawi and Bahai are all offshoots of the Shiites.

Under the first caliphs the seat of power was Mecca, but then it moved to Damascus under the Umayyad dynasty (638-750 CE). During this period the Holy Land thrived as can be seen from the archaeological remains of palaces in Jerusalem and Jericho. In 750 CE the (Sunni) Umayyads were overthrown by the (Shiite) Abbasids and the center of power shifted to Baghdad.

"Al Walid beheld Syria to be a country that had long been occupied by the Christians, and he noted herein the beautiful churches still belonging to them, so enchantingly fair, and so renowned for their splendour, even as are the Kumamah [the Church of the Holy Sepulchre at Jerusalem], and the churches of Lydda and Edessa. So he sought to build for the Muslims a mosque that should prevent their regarding these, and that should be unique and a wonder to the world. And in like manner is it not evident how the Khalif Abd el Malik, noting the greatness of the Dome of the Kumamah [the Holy Sepulcher] and its magnificence, was moved lest it should dazzle the minds of the Muslims, and hence erected above the Rock, the Dome which now is seen there!"

Mukaddasi, 985 CE
(Guy Le Strange, *Palestine under the Moslems* [London, 1890; repr., New York: AMS Press, 1975], 117)

Dome of the Rock in Jerusalem

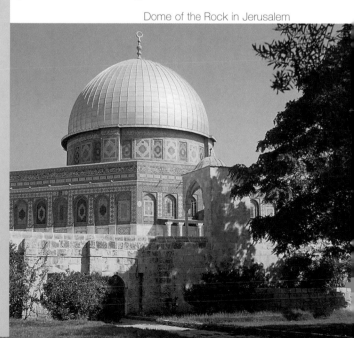

Mosque at Ramla

One of the notable Abbasid caliphs, Haroun al-Rashid (783-809 CE), made an alliance with Charlemagne of France (later to become Holy Roman emperor) and presented him with the keys to the Church of the Resurrection which was under Muslim control.

The Abbasid hegemony was disrupted in the tenth century with the creation of the (Shiite) Fatimid caliphate in Egypt which extended its rule to include the Holy Land and destroyed many churches. During the rule of al-Hakim (996-1021 CE) a group broke away from the Ismailia Shiites.

Persecuted in Egypt in the eighteenth century, they eventually settled in the remote hills of Galilee, Golan Heights and Syria. Known as Druze, they practiced a secret religion, which has no similarity to Islam, and venerated their prophet Jethro at the tomb of Nebi Shueb.

The population of the Holy Land continued to decrease, agriculture diminishing, vineyards destroyed. Absentee landowners taxed the peasants who barely eked out a living. Desolation and lawlessness prevailed, travel was dangerous, pilgrims were attacked. The rivalry between the caliphates made the Holy Land ripe for Crusader conquest.

The Muslim conquest of the Holy Land took a number of years. Jerusalem was conquered by Caliph Omar in 638 after a two-year siege. Mujir a-Din describes in 1496 that Omar looked for the Rock on the Temple Mount on which the Temple had stood. He found it covered with centuries of rubbish and ordered it cleaned. It was he who determined that a mosque would be built south of the stone.

In the Holy Land the administrative areas of the Byzantine Empire were unchanged. Palaestina Prima became Jund Falastin (as there is no *P* in Arabic it is replaced with an *F*) with its capital in Lydda, until it was moved to Ramla,

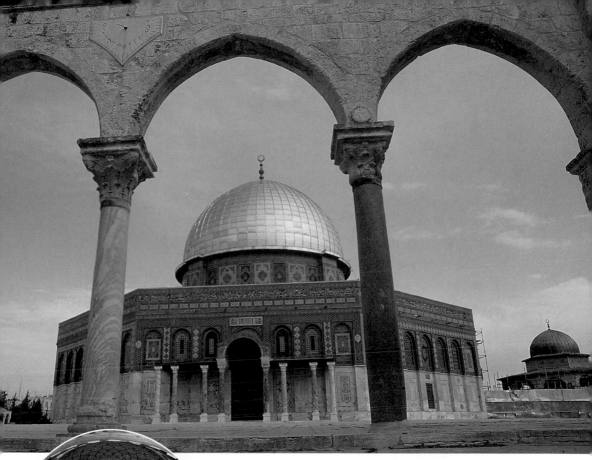

Exterior and interior views of the Dome of the Rock in Jerusalem

"Then 'Abd al Malik forbade the people of Syria to make the pilgrimage [to Mecca].... This Rock, of which it is reported that upon it the Apostle of Allah set his foot when he ascended to heaven, shall be unto you in the place of the Ka'abah."

Ya'kubi, 891 CE
(Le Strange, *Palestine under the Moslems,* 116)

the only city to be built in the Arab period. Palaestina Secunda became Jund al-Urdunn with its capital in Tiberias. (Jund al-Urdunn is the Jordan River district).

The importance of Jerusalem declined and is barely mentioned in early Muslim annals.

The Dome of the Rock, built on the Temple Mount in Jerusalem, is the best-known site of the Early Arab period. Built in 691 CE by Umayyad Caliph Abd al-Malik, it was a memorial honoring the rock on which it was built, the rock from which Muhammad ascended to heaven. According to the legend, the Rock tried to ascend with him only to be pushed back by the angel Gabriel and visitors are shown

Hisham's palace in Jericho

Muhammad's footprint and the imprint of Gabriel's hand.

The inspiration for the design of the Dome of the Rock was the rotunda of the nearby Byzantine Church of the Resurrection. The dome, which collapsed in 1016, has been repaired many times, gold leafed in 1962 and again in 1994. The facade tiles have been replaced, but the original structure is unchanged.

The interior is decorated with geometric and floral patterns and inscriptions in stylized Arabic, mainly from the Koran. Abbasid Caliph al-Mamun erased the name of al-Malik, the builder, and replaced it with his own. Because he omitted to change the date, his forgery was exposed.

There is no mention of Jerusalem in the Koran. In the verses referring to Muhammad's night flight on his horse, al-Burak, the destination is given as el-Aksa (the furthest) Mosque, originally thought to have been heaven.

The Umayyads, who moved the center of Islamic rule to Damascus, needed a Muslim pilgrimage site to compete with Mecca and Medina. At this point the "Furthest Mosque" was redefined as Jerusalem, already holy to Jews and Christians.

Caliph al-Walid, 709-715 CE, built the el-Aksa Mosque at the southern end of the Temple Mount on the site of the Byzantine Church of St. Mary. This mosque underwent many changes and even served as a church in the Crusader period.

In Philip Hitti's classic *A History of the Arabs*, these two sites, the Dome of the Rock and the el-Aksa Mosque, are the only ones mentioned in the entire Holy Land area. Jerusalem, however, did not gain religious importance in Islamic tradition and did not become a major pilgrimage site.

Although there is no record of the Umayyad palace outside the southern wall of the Temple Mount, archaeological excavations have uncovered this previously unknown luxurious complex.

A short distance from Jericho another Umayyad palace, Khirbat Mafjar, has been excavated. Built by the caliph Hisham ibn Abd el-Malik (724-743 CE) and razed by an earthquake, probably before it was much used, the beautiful mosaics and many statues of human and animal figures indicate a pre-iconoclastic (destruction of images) period in Muslim art.

The masons' symbols on the stones are in Hebrew, indicating Jewish builders. The remains of the "Shalom al Israel" synagogue close by confirm that there was a large Jewish population in the vicinity. Mukaddasi described the minaret built by Hisham and defined the *mihrab* (prayer niche) as the most beautiful in all Islam. Sections of the intricate water system have been excavated.

At this time Arabic was introduced as an official language, alongside Greek which, in a short time, was no longer used.

The importance of Jerusalem declined — in fact only two Abbasid caliphs visited Jerusalem. The area west of the Jordan River was now known as Jund Falastin (a corruption of the Byzantine Palaestina) and its administrative capital was the new town of Ramla, built in 718 CE on the main trade route between Egypt and Damascus.

During the tenth and eleventh centuries the Muslim empire was rife with internecine wars. As in the Hellenistic period, over a thousand years earlier, once again the Holy Land became the fought-over buffer zone. In 979 the Fatamids of Egypt extended their rule only to be repulsed by the Abbasids. Taking advantage of this rivalry, one of the Bedouin tribes temporarily established its own autonomous independence in parts of the Holy Land. Arab rule ended with the conquest of Baghdad, Damascus and then the Holy Land by the Seljuks, a Turkish tribe from Asia Minor. Fatimid Egypt was now threatened.

The Byzantine Empire in Asia shrunk until only Constantinople, the capital, remained. The Papal Bull of 1054 had resulted in the final and complete schism between the Catholic and Orthodox Churches so the Roman Empire did not immediately rally to assist the Byzantine Empire against the Seljuk encroachment in Asia Minor.

In the Holy Land, over the centuries the population had diminished as the economic situation deteriorated. This was partly due to the decrease in agriculture, in particular the destruction of the vineyards. The markets of Europe were no longer available. Absentee landlords taxed peasants who barely eked out a living. Desolation and lawlessness prevailed, travel was dangerous, pilgrims were attacked.

Aerial view of Haram al-Sharif (aka the Temple Mount) with the golden Dome of the Rock in the center. To the right is the southern excavation. On the top the Mary Magdalene and Dominus Flevit churches and the cemetery on the Mount of Olives. In the center, the Western Wall.

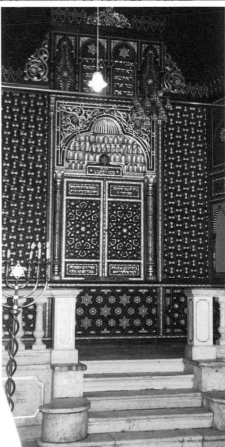

The Ezra-Synagogue in Cairo, where an extensive eighth-to eleventh-century archive was found

Much was learned of the hardships of the tenth and eleventh centuries (and onwards) as well as of the political upheavals that affected the Holy Land from documents and correspondence found in the Ezra Synagogue archives, in Fostat (Cairo). Discovered by chance in the late nineteenth century and brought to Cambridge University, they are still being researched and published. One of the more important finds was the earliest copy of the Tanach (Hebrew Scriptures) then known.

In addition to the many Jewish communities there was also a flourishing Karaite community in Egypt and at least two synagogues in Ramla. Karaites follow the biblical law but do not recognize the Oral Law as binding.

To a large extent it was the rivalry between the caliphates that made the Holy Land ripe for the Crusader conquest.

CRUSADER KINGDOMS

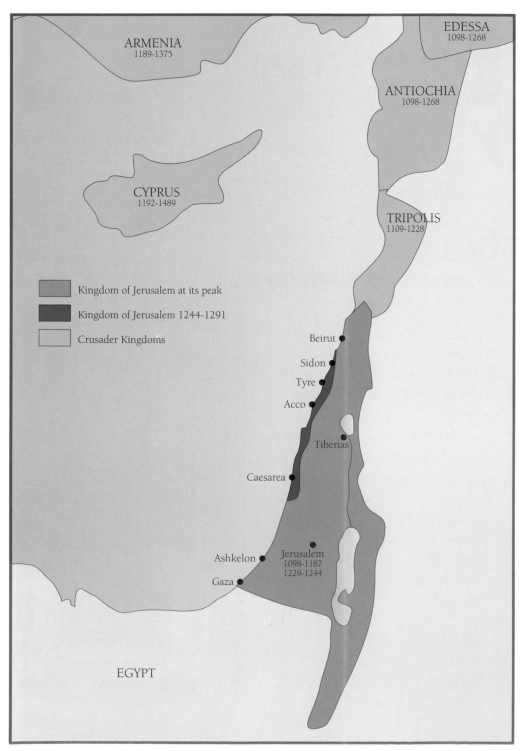

ARMENIA
1189-1375

EDESSA
1098-1268

ANTIOCHIA
1098-1268

CYPRUS
1192-1489

TRIPOLIS
1109-1228

Kingdom of Jerusalem at its peak

Kingdom of Jerusalem 1244-1291

Crusader Kingdoms

Beirut

Sidon

Tyre

Acco

Tiberias

Caesarea

Ashkelon

Jerusalem
1098-1187
1229-1244

Gaza

EGYPT

CHAPTER 8

1099-1291 Crusader Period

> "Whoever, therefore , shall determine on this holy pilgrimage and shall make his vow to God to that effect and shall offer himself to Him as a living sacrifice, holy, acceptable to God, shall wear the sign of the cross of the Lord on his forehead or on his breast."
>
> *Pope Urban II, Speech at Council of Clermont, 1095 CE*

The rivalry between Fatamid Egypt and the Seljuk Turks for the control of the Holy Land resulted in a power vacuum. Together with obstacles placed in the way of Christian pilgrims, the stage was set for the Crusader conquest.

In Europe too there was upheaval. Independent kings and princes were constantly at war with one another. In an attempt to unify Europe (which, together with England, was Catholic) the pope called for a combined crusade to free the Christian holy places from the infidel. Pope Urban II had another motive. The outcome of the papal bull of 1054 was the final and complete schism between the Catholic and Orthodox Churches. As the Orthodox Byzantine (Greek) Empire refused to accept the authority of the pope and the supremacy of the Catholic Church, Orthodox Christians were excluded from Catholic communion. In retaliation Rome was excommunicated by the Orthodox. Urban II hoped to force the Byzantine Empire (which was Orthodox) to recognize Rome as the leader of the Christian world.

Who were the crusaders who answered this call? On one hand feudal knights, usually the third son, who could not inherit family property in Europe and England, with nothing to lose and perhaps

honor to gain. On the other hand, the peasants and rabble, unemployed and starving in many cases. They had everything to gain including a church pardon for all sins, past, present and future.

It is doubtful whether the Crusaders ever comprised more than 25 percent of the population in the areas they conquered in the Holy Land.

The local population consisted mainly of:

1. Arab peasants who leased the land from absentee landlords and, after paying taxes, barely eked out a living (Arabs in the cities were slaughtered by the conquering crusaders)

2. Jews in towns and villages throughout the land

3. Various Christian communities, none of whom were Catholic.

During their rule, the Crusaders stepped into the place of the absentee landlords and imposed European feudal law, which probably improved the conditions of the peasants. The Jewish population was persecuted and even banned from Jerusalem.

No close relations were formed with the local Christian population. Often the Crusaders replaced the Greek Orthodox, Syrian Jacobite, Armenian, Coptic and Ethiopian Bishops and clergy with Latin (Catholic) prelates. Instead of a Christian alliance, these groups even saw Saladin as their savior.

The demise of Crusader rule was partly due to the lack of unity among the crusaders themselves. But their final expulsion was due to the changes in the area.

The arches supporting the southern platform of the Temple Mount area — known in the Crusader period as Templum Solomon — now used by Muslim worshippers as an extension to the el-Aksa Mosque

Crusades

Crusader "Double Cross" used to carry relics

Between 1095 and 1297 there were a number of Crusades to the Holy Land. Not all of them reached its shores. Their initial successes were partly due to the continuing rivalry between the Seljuks in the north and the Fatimids in Egypt, who did not appreciate the Crusader threat to their presence in the Holy Land.

The First Crusade (1095-99) established princedoms in Antiochia and Edessa and, under Tancred and Godfrey de Bouillon, the first king, finally conquered Jerusalem in 1099.

William of Tyre described the conquest of Jerusalem: "It was impossible to look upon the vast numbers of slain without horror; everywhere lay fragments of human bodies, and the very ground was covered with the blood of the slain. It was not alone the spectacle of the headless bodies and mutilated limbs strewn in all directions that roused horror in all who looked upon them. Still more dreadful it was to gaze upon the victors themselves, dripping with blood from head to foot."

After the conquest of Jerusalem, many of the crusaders returned to Europe. Baldwin succeeded Godfrey as king. Over the next forty years the Crusader kingdom consolidated and reached a modus vivendi with the Muslim emirs,

Church of St. Anne at the pools of Bethesda

including those of Damascus, Aleppo and Hamat. Those of Damascus preferred an alliance with the Crusaders rather than one with Zengi of Mosul, which was under Seljuk rule. (The Iraqis taunt the Syrians about this right up to the present!)

The fleets of Genoa, Venice and Pisa were offered concessions — customs exemptions and commerical monopolies — for their assistance. All the coastal cities from Beirut and Sidon in the north down to Ashkelon in the south came under Crusader control.

Assisted by the Crusaders, the Damascenes repulsed Zengi. As a reward, Banias was ceded by the Syrians to the Crusaders. But this alliance didn't last long. In 1144 the Crusader princedom of Edessa fell to Zengi. Antiochia was in danger. Mobilization for the Second Crusade now began. The Crusader attempt to secure Damascus failed and Damascus fell to Nuradin, Zengi's heir.

In the south the Crusaders attempted to conquer Egypt. To halt their advance Fostat (Cairo) was razed by Saladin, commander of the Egyptian forces. In 1171 the Shiite Fatimid dynasty in Egypt came to an end, and with her recognition of the caliphate of Baghdad, Egypt too became Sunni.

Saladin, a Kurd from Iraq, became ruler of Egypt. The Crusader kingdom was a buffer zone between the two rivals — Nuradin and Saladin. Saladin's attempt to attack the kingdom of Jerusalem resulted in his defeat at the hands of Amalric and realization that he had to unite the Muslims from North Africa to Turkey, Egypt, Aleppo and Damascus.

During this period the Crusaders did not reorganize and Europe sent no reinforcements. England and France were at war, Germany and the papacy were at loggerheads, Spain was occupied with the Muslim invasion. Possibly too the failure of the Second Crusade had left its mark. The fateful battle of the Horns of Hittin in July 1187 was the beginning of the end for the Crusader kingdom.

The Crusaders were at Sepphoris (Zippori) when they heard of the fall of Tiberias. Count Raymond, a Hospitaller knight whose ancestors arrived on the First Crusade, urged his colleagues not to be lured into a battle where the Crusader army would be short of water. Gerard of Ridefort, a Templar and relative newcomer, convinced the weak Guy de Lusignan to attack at once to regain Tiberias.

Crusader fortress at Sepphoris (Zippori)

Walls of Acco (Acre)

Because Muslim horsemen were lightly armed they had more maneuverability than the heavily armored mounted knights. The Crusaders set out for Tiberias but by afternoon had only covered eighteen kilometers. They had suffered heavy losses and were without water. Raymond suggested that the Crusaders detour immediately to the springs of Hattin, five kilometers away, in order to obtain water and regroup. Guy decided to set up camp and rest till morning.

This gave the Muslims ample time to reorganize their troops and to bring water and supplies from the rear, harassing the Crusaders all the while. In the morning the Crusaders tried to get to the Hattin Springs but Saladin succeeded in separating the mounted knights from their protective shield of foot soldiers and then set fire to the dry grass.

The Crusaders fought valiantly but to no avail. The true cross, brought from Jerusalem, was captured; the leaders were imprisoned and the kingdom was now defenseless. In October 1187 Jerusalem fell to Saladin. The Crusader kingdom shrank to a narrow strip along the coastal plain.

In Europe the Third Crusade was mobilized, led by Frederick I, Phillip II and Richard the Lionhearted. Cyprus was conquered. In the Holy Land the battle at Acco was the most notable. The Crusader forces, under Guy de Lusignan, had laid siege to the town. They were in turn encircled by the Muslim forces of Saladin. After two years the starved city surrendered in 1211. Richard then defeated Saladin at Arsuf and they signed a treaty at Ramla establishing the truncated second kingdom of Jerusalem, which lasted only for ten years.

The Fourth Crusade, which failed to take advantage of the dissolution of the united empire of Saladin when he died, and the slow demise of the Ayyub dynasty

Walls and gateway at Caesarea

he had founded, and chose instead to conquer got no further than Constantinople. The aim of the Fifth Crusade was to conquer Egypt and resulted in an agreement with the Egyptian sultan. Then, due to hostility between the rulers of Egypt and Damascus, the Sixth Crusade was planned, to be led by Emperor Friedrich II. When he postponed his departure he was excommunicated by the pope. He finally arrived in 1228. After negotiations with the Egyptian sultan the size of the Crusader kingdom was enlarged to include Jerusalem, excluding the Temple Mount itself. Friedrich was crowned king of Jerusalem at the Church of the Holy Sepulcher. The coronation was boycotted by the Church, apart from the Teutonic Order.

The factionalized Crusader kingdom was unable to take advantage of the equally divided Muslim world. Reinforced by tribes that were displaced as Genghis Khan advanced from Mongolia, the Egyptian army captured Jerusalem in 1244. The entire Christian population was massacred.

Fired by the loss of Jerusalem, Louis IX led a French Crusade, which like the Fifth, hoped to conquer Egypt. Routed by Sultan al-Malik Baybars, commander of the Egyptian mercenaries, Louis was forced to withdraw but succeeded in regaining almost all of the Holy Land. After a short interlude it shrank once again to a narrow coastal strip.

Led by Baybars, the Mamelukes, as the tribal slaves who made up the mercenary army that served the Egyptian sultan were known, overthrew their masters, the last of the Ayyubids, descendants of Saladin, and gained control of Egypt, to the west. The Mongols, led by Genghis Khan, captured Damascus, to the northeast, and in their advance to Egypt were stopped at Ein Jalud (Ein Harod springs) in 1260 by the Mamelukes.

The crusaders were caught in between. One after another the Crusader strongholds and cities fell until finally, when Acco fell in 1291, the Crusader kingdom was completely destroyed by the Mamelukes.

The Seventh, and last, Crusade, the Children's Crusade, didn't even leave the shores of Europe. The children either died or were sold as slaves.

Left: Abu-Ghosh Church
Below: The archaeological site of Emmaus

Aerial view of Belvoir which overlooks the Jordan River

Catholic Orders

One of the outcomes of the Crusades was the creation of various orders. Initially these were military orders which spread through Europe and became religious in their character.

The Knights of St. John, or the Hospitallers, provided hostels and hospitals for the pilgrims visiting the holy places, as well as serving as an armed guard on their perilous journey.

The Order of the Templars guarded the Temple of Solomon, which replaced the el-Aksa Mosque on the Temple Mount. The Carmelite Order to this day has two monasteries on Mount Carmel, recalling the prophet Elijah's challenge to the prophets of Baal and Ashtoret in the Kingdom of Israel and the threat to his life by King Ahab and his wife Jezebel.

The Lazarist Order devoted itself to taking care of lepers. The Teutons were the only order which was not international and was made up of only German-speaking knights. The largest order in the Holy Land today is the Franciscan Order (founded by St. Francis of Assisi), who are the custodians of the Catholic holy sites.

A detailed record of the Jewish population is to be found in the travel diary of Benjamin of Tudelah who not only records the size of the community but also the professions and trades they practice. Rabbi Nachmanides (the Ramban), who was forced to leave Spain after his disputation with the Church, moved to Jerusalem. Many Jewish sages, fleeing the Inquisition, settled around Acco.

Many of the Crusader remains throughout the country, such as Belvoir, Acco (Acre), Kal'at Nimrod, Caesarea and Montfort, date to the final swan song of the Crusader kingdom. Their size and majesty belie the fact that the Crusaders were overcome by internal disputes and lacked unity or a forceful command.

Churches that the Crusaders had built, sometimes on the ruins of Byzantine churches (destroyed during the early Muslim rule), were destroyed by the new Muslim conquerers. In the Church of the Multiplication at Tabgha, Church of the Annunciation in Nazareth, the Church of the Transfiguration on Mount Tabor, the Tomb of Lazarus, St. Anne and the Dormition Church, among others, some architects have tried to incorporate earlier ruins in the modern churches.

Aerial view of Mount Tabor with the Church of the Transfiguration and the Crusader excavations

CHAPTER 9

1291-1517 Mameluke Period

The Mameluke period overlaps the end of the Crusader period, with its ever-decreasing kingdom. The Mamelukes were not a people or a nation. They were the descendants of pagan slaves brought from Asia Minor by the caliphs of Egypt, to serve in their personal armies. In time they usurped power and became the rulers of Egypt.

In 1260 the Mamelukes under Sultan al-Malik Baybars stopped the advance of Mongol tribes, united under Genghis Khan, at the battle of Ein Jalud (Ein Harod). Syria came under Mameluke control and the Crusader kingdom was caught in between, shrinking until it was merely the coastal strip and then, finally, vanquished.

To prevent the return of the Crusaders, harbors were filled with the rubble of the razed cities and citadels. Baybars is quoted as saying: "Your ships are your horses and our horses are our ships."

Opposite page: Nimrod's Fortress.
Left: View of mosque in Acco

"Oh, if only you had seen your knights trampled by our horses, your houses looted...your women sold in the market place...your churches utterly destroyed...the tombs of the patriarchs trodden underfoot...your Muslim enemy trampling down your altars and holy of holies, cutting the throats of deacons, priests and bishops...your soul would have expired with sighs, and the multitude of your tears would have quenched the devouring flame."

Excerpts from a letter from Sultan Baybars to Bohemond VI, Prince of Antioch, May 1268 (Robert Payne, *The Dream and the Tomb* [New York: Dorset Press,1984], 370)

Harbor at Acco

This destruction led to the abandonment of entire areas along the coastal strip. Discharged soldiers, mainly from Egypt, were resettled further inland.

The Mameluke capital, Cairo, was not in the center of the empire, so an elaborate early warning system was devised. A report from northern Syria could reach Cairo in sixty hours. The road system was improved, bridges were built and a chain of khans, at regular intervals, were provided with relief horses. At the entrance to Lod one such bridge is still in use, with the engraving of a lion amusing itself with a mouse — the symbol used by Baybars.

To counter the dangers of a new crusade and to control Christian pilgrims, the Islamic aspects of the province were emphasized. In Ramla, the Great Mosque, which had been converted to a church, was renovated. The Red Mosque was built in Safed and residents of Damascus were encouraged to emigrate to Safed by gifts of fertile lands in the surrounding valleys.

During the rule of the Calhoun dynasty in Egypt the Holy Land was once more divided into administrative areas, with capitals at Gaza and Safed. During this period the terms Palaestina or Falastin are not used at all.

The Cave of the Machpela (the tomb of the patriarchs and the matriarchs) in Hebron was renovated and entry to non-Muslims was barred — a ban which continued until 1967. On the Temple Mount the el-Aksa Mosque was repaired and enlarged and a public water fountain was built. In Ramla the White Mosque was built. Gaza was transformed from a village to a bustling town.

In order to express loyalty to Muslim culture, the Mamelukes built extensively in Jerusalem. All the buildings were consecrated to the Muslim authorities. In this way they safeguarded the future of their sons who, by law, were not allowed to inherit their father's rank, possessions or position.

Legally, the sultan was permitted to confiscate the possessions of a Mameluke for the state treasury. However, as no sultan could confiscate holy endowments, by appointing their sons as trustees of property bequeathed to the Wakf (Muslim religious authorities), they were thereby guaranteed a regular income. Their striking white, pink and black stone buildings can still be seen in the Old City of Jerusalem.

Although they built beautifully, they did not govern well. Most of the time the country was in chaos and Bedouin tribes marauded at will. Travel was dangerous. The custom of wealth and influence being monopolized by a handful of families gained ground.

Officials in Damascus and Cairo, doubtless on receipt of a generous tribute from these families, authorized the acquisition of large land holdings and their appointment to the most influential political and religious offices in the province. As the economic situation worsened the population continued to decrease. Agriculture was merely subsistence farming. The land was truly laid to waste.

During most of the Mameluke period the custodians of the Christian holy places were the Franciscans. Their headquarters were at the Cenacle on Mount Zion, which they had purchased from the Egyptian sultan in 1332. However, those few sites which had not been destroyed at the end of the Crusader period were generally in a very poor state of repair.

The beginning of the demise of the Mameluke Empire began in 1453, when Mehmed II of the expanding Ottoman Empire seized Constantinople and gained control of most of what was once the Byzantine Empire. The Ottoman Turks proceeded to usurp the caliphate from the Mamelukes and by 1517 the Holy Land was formally under Ottoman rule.

Khan el Umdan, Acco

CHAPTER 10

1517-1917 Ottoman Period

Once again we see how events in other parts of the world affect the Holy Land. The Mongols, the Seljuks and now the Ottoman Turks, who exploited the power vacuum in what remained of the Byzantine Empire, penetrated Western Europe. Their rule extended almost as far as Vienna, included the Balkans, Eastern Europe, the Black Sea, North Africa, Egypt and Asia as far as Persia. Even the Muslim holy cities of Mecca and Medina recognized Ottoman control.

Suleiman the Magnificent, builder of the present-day walls of the Old City of Jerusalem, offered asylum to Jews who had been expelled in 1492 from Spain. Many of them made their way to Safed in the Galilee, which became the center of kabala studies. For a short while, Tiberias thrived under the influence of Donna Gracia and her nephew Don Joseph Nasi.

Opposite page: Jerusalem by David Roberts
Below: The Damascus Gate, one of the gates in the walls of the Old City, built by Suleiman II c. 1537

The minaret of the Citadel, adjoining the Jaffa Gate, sometimes incorrectly known as the Tower of David

France, the protector of the Catholic churches and holy places in the Holy Land, was the first to penetrate the Ottoman Empire as it began to weaken. Then the Russians became the protectors of the Orthodox churches throughout the Ottoman Empire.

For a short period in the mid-eighteenth century, Daher el-Omar took control of the Galilee area and improved the condition of the local population by developing agriculture and even encouraging Jewish settlement. He was overthrown by Ahmed Pasha el-Jazzar who, assisted by his private army of Albanian, Bosnian and Circassian mercenaries, governed from Acco.

In 1798, Napoleon invaded Egypt, realizing that it was the key to the east. Continuing up the Mediterranean coast, the French reached Jaffa, where they offered terms of surrender. These were either rejected, resulting in wholesale looting and massacre, or were accepted and then ignored by the French who, due to manpower shortage, could not afford to use their meager troops for guards and so marched the captives straight into the sea.

The French were beset by plagues but continued their conquests through Samaria and Galilee, hoping to advance to Constantinople and thus into Europe from the east. Unbeknownst to them, el-Jezzar of Acco was assisted by Col. Phillippe, a Frenchman who had been at the military academy with Napoleon, but was now fighting with the English.

Cannon on Jaffa promenade; in the background, modern Tel Aviv

"Abdallah Pasha of [Acre] caused great mischief to the Christians.... He demanded such great sums of money that the payment left them both impoverished and in serious straits. He...continued to threaten...them until they finally escaped to the mountains of the Lebanon.... When the Pasha arrived in Jerusalem... [he] sent soldiers who plundered the monastery." After taking possession of Jerusalem, Mohammed Ali, viceroy of Egypt, sent Ibrahim Pasha with a large army against Abdullah Pasha. "Meeting with no resistance Ibrahim took Gaza, Jaffa, Jerusalem, Samaria and all Galilee." During the six-month siege of Acre, the walls of the town, the houses and palaces were destroyed. "The conquest of [Acre] was celebrated in Jerusalem with illuminations, dancing, and music.... All were happy and delighted at the thought that Egyptian entry meant freedom."
Monk Neophitos of Cyprus (Extracts from Annals of Palestine, 1821-1841 [Jerusalem: Ariel, 1979], 29)

The siege and assault on Acco failed and with the English fleet in the Mediterranean the French had no option but to retreat the way they had come — to Egypt and then back to France.

A little-known proclamation issued by Napoleon, addressed to "the rightful heirs of Palestine" called on the "Israelites, unique nation, whom, in thousands of years, lust of conquest were able to deprive of the ancestral lands only, but not of name and national existence" to "claim the restoration of your rights among the population of the universe."

In 1831, Muhammad Ali extended Egypt's borders to include Palestine. During his rule, and that of his son Ibrahim Pasha, many Egyptians settled in the Holy Land. In 1841, an alliance of England, Prussia, Austria and Turkey returned Palestine to the Ottoman Empire, which henceforth would be known as the "sick man of Europe."

Holy Places

Prior to the Turkish conquest of the Holy Land in 1517, the Franciscans had been the custodians of the Christian holy places. In 1552 Suleiman ejected them from the Cenacle, which came under Muslim control. The scope of influence of the Orthodox Church was increased and care of the holy places passed from the Catholic Church to the Orthodox Church.

Possession of the holy places would henceforth be in the forefront of international politics. The French ambassador to the Ottoman Empire represented the interests of the Catholic Church. In 1774 Russia officially became the protector of the sultan's Orthodox subjects. (England would later assume the position of protector of the Jewish subjects.)

As the weakened Turkey was forced into "capitulations," ownership of such places as the Church of the Holy Sepulchre swung from Catholic to Orthodox and back like a pendulum. After the fire of 1808, which destroyed the Rotunda and Crusader building over the Tomb, the present shrine over the Tomb was constructed by the Orthodox, who also repaired the church, thereby gaining control of most of it.

France, on behalf of Sardinia, Belgium, Spain and Austria, demanded that the holy places revert to Catholic control. Russia objected strongly. In 1852 Sultan Abdul Mejid issued a *firman* (royal decree) rejecting the French demands and directed that the status quo be maintained.

In the subsequent war against Russia, Turkey was assisted by England, France and Sardinia. The Treaty of Paris in 1855, which ended the Crimean War, upheld the status quo. From the close of the nineteenth century new churches and hospices were built both within and outside the walls of Jerusalem as well as at holy sites throughout the Holy Land.

One of the pretexts for the Crimean War (1853-56) related to guardianship of the Christian holy places in Palestine. Turkey declared war on Russia, the protector of the Orthodox Church. France, protector of the Catholic Church, and England joined Turkey. In return, the Western powers were henceforth going to be awarded "capitulations" in Palestine, which was slowly awakening from a six-hundred-year-long deep sleep.

Most of the land throughout the Ottoman Empire belonged to the sultan who often put it at the disposal of an influential class of absentee landlords. In some areas pasturing and wood gathering was permitted to all, but this resulted in the deterioration of the quality of the soil. By and large the local Muslim population were peasants living in abject poverty and paying exhorbitant taxes to absentee landlords.

Opposite page: The church and monastery of Notre Dame, located outside the walls of the Old City

The windmill adjoining the first neighborhoods outside the city walls of Jerusalem, built by Sir Moses Montefiore

Jews lived mainly in Jerusalem, Hebron, Tiberias and Safed — known as the four holy cities — as well as in Jaffa, the only port of entry to Palestine. For many, their existence depended on donations from abroad, such as the support of Moses Montefiore (later Sir Moses), who built the first residential neighborhood outside the walls of Jerusalem.

In 1864, in Springfield, Massachusetts, a group of Christians led by George Jones Adams decided to establish a colony in Palestine, there to await the second advent of the Messiah. One hundred fifty-three followers arrived in 1866 and the prefabricated houses they brought with them can still be seen in Jaffa, where they settled.

Unfortunately they were left destitute by their leader and Mark Twain, on a cruise in the Mediterranean, collected money from his companions to repatriate those who so desired. Only twenty-nine remained, and one of them would drive the first carriage on the first paved road.

Mark Twain described the land as a "desolate country whose soil is rich enough, but is given over wholly to weeds — a silent mournful expanse.... A desolation is here that not even imagination can grace with the pomp of life and action ... even the olive and the cactus, those fast friends of a worthless soil, [have] almost deserted the country" (*Innocents Abroad*, 1867).

At about the same time, another Christian group was organized in Germany for the same religious reason. Known as the Templars, they established a number of colonies, introduced modern agricultural equipment, constructed the first roads and signed a contract with Thomas Cook, thereby establishing the first travel agency in Palestine.

In 1868, the Bahu'allah, founder of the Bahai faith, was exiled to

> "There is not a solitary village throughout [the] whole extent [of the Jezre'el Valley].... Come to Galilee... that melancholy ruin of Capernaum; this stupid village of Tiberias.... We reached Tabor safely.... We never saw a human being on the whole route.... Nazareth is forlorn.... Jericho the accursed lies a mouldering ruin today, even as Joshua's miracle left it more than three thousand years ago; Bethlehem and Bethany, in their poverty and their humiliation, have nothing to remind one that they once knew the high honor of the Saviour's presence."
>
> Mark Twain, *Innocents Abroad*

The Bahai shrine and gardens in Haifa

Acco, where he is buried. The Bab, herald of the faith, was reinterred in Haifa. These shrines are regarded as holy places and are visited by Bahai pilgrims from all over the world.

The opening of the Suez Canal in 1869 put Palestine firmly on the tourist map thanks to the many VIPs who attended the opening ceremony and then continued to the Holy Land. The Ottoman Empire was obliged to invest first in the road from Jaffa to Jerusalem and then a road from the coast to Nazareth.

"The [German] colonists were almost without exception men of very moderate means...engaged in a severe and unequal struggle. They persevere[d] with the most unflinching resolution [pand established settlements in Jaffa, Haifa, Sarona and Jerusalem.] ... Perhaps the most remarkable innovation is the introduction of wheeled vehicles. Fifteen years ago (1869) a cart had never been seen by the inhabitants of Haifa."

Laurence Oliphant, *Haifa, or Life in Modern Palestine*, Elibron Classics Series (Edinburgh and London: William Blackwood and Sons, 1887; Chestnut Hill, MA: Adamant Media Corporation, 2005), 19, 20

The very first wave of Jewish immigration is one that is generally forgotten — Jews from Yemen who made their way by foot, nourished by religious fervor.

After them came the East European Jews of the First Aliya (immigration). Members of different organizations encouraged the return of the Jewish people to the land where they had originated. Many were religious families.

Under the leadership of Theodore Herzl, representatives of these groups met at the First Zionist Congress in 1897 in Basel. There, Herzl prophesied that the Jews would have their own state within fifty years: "If you will it, it is no dream."

Opposite page: While Jewish, Christian, Muslim and Bahai sites are familiar to many visitors, few know the Achmedian mosque in Haifa. Achmedians consider themselves to be Muslims who do not believe in religious war (jihad). However, they are not recognized by the Muslim world.

This page: Buildings in the Old City of Safed

Money collected throughout the Jewish world helped to finance the purchase of land for the many settlements as well as for schools and even the beginnings of a bank. The farming colonies established then are towns of modern Israel — Rishon LeZion, Petach Tikva, Rosh Pina, Zichron Ya'acov, to name but a few.

The land offered for sale was in uncultivated areas, mainly the valleys which more often than not were malaria-infested swamps. H. B. Tristram did not find "a sign of habitation...in the valleys, even where the valley is wide, fertile and suitable for cultivation...a monotony of stagnation, devoid of life and movement" (*The Land of Israel: A Journal of Travels in Palestine*, 1865).

In many instances, it was the generosity of Baron Edmond Rothschild that helped the pioneers survive such hardships as shortage of water and illness. He was successful in reintroducing the wine industry to the Holy Land. The mulberry trees in Rosh Pina were to serve as a base for the silk farms, but this plan did not succeed.

In 1892, the first railway line was completed. Instead of it taking a full day to reach Jerusalem from Jaffa, it now took only a few hours. (It still takes a few hours to get to Jerusalem by train, following the same winding, scenic route. Even the Jerusalem railway station is unchanged!)

Turkey was interested in completing the Hejaz line to connect Turkey with the Muslim sites at Mecca and Medina. The various branch lines connecting Haifa, Tiberias, Beit Shean, Afula and on to Be'er Sheva were important for the development of the country.

1904 saw the beginning of a new wave of immigration, the Second Aliya. This consisted mainly of young people, shocked by the Kishinev pogroms and disillusioned by the first Russian Revolution, but fired with the idea of socialism.

These were the pioneers who would establish the kibbutz and moshav movements and introduce a form of settlement based on a communal lifestyle and mutual responsibility. Right up until today, people all over the world volunteer to work on a kibbutz in order to experience this unique way of life.

The economic development in an island of stagnation caused Arabs from the neighboring provinces of the Ottoman Empire to come to Palestine in search of work. They came from as far afield as Algeria and Libya in North Africa and Syria to the east.

The outbreak of World War I in 1914 brought an economic crisis. Palestine was completely cut off and not even mail, and with it donations, got through. Fearing mobilization by the Turkish army, many fled. Non-Turks were exiled to Tiberias, or worse, to Turkey.

A small group of people, led by Aaron Aaronsohn, the agronomist who traced the domestication of wild wheat, and his sister Sarah, formed an espionage unit known as Netzach Israel Lo Yishaker

Kibbutz Mishmar HaEmek, one of the pioneer kibbutzim in the Jezre'el Valley, founded in 1922. It played an integral role in the establishment of the State of Israel and in the War of Independence.

("the Strength of Israel will not lie," I Sam 15:29), abbreviated to NILI. They collected and transmitted information to the British forces in Cairo.

Even prior to the end of the war, France and Britain had divided the Ottoman Empire between them by the Sykes-Picot Agreement. Under General Allenby, later Palestine was conquered by Britain. At the same time, Lord Balfour, in a letter to Lord Rothschild, promised the Jewish people a "national home" in Palestine.

With these events the Ottoman period draws to a close.

"His Majesty's Government view with favour the establishment in Palestine of a national home for the Jewish people, and will use their best endeavours to facilitate the achievement of this object, it being clearly understood that nothing shall be done which may prejudice the civil and religious rights of existing non-Jewish communities in Palestine, or the rights and political status enjoyed by Jews in any other country."

From a letter to Lord Rothschild by Lord Arthur James Balfour, Secretary of State, British Foreign Office, November 2, 1917

MIDDLE EAST AFTER WORLD WAR I

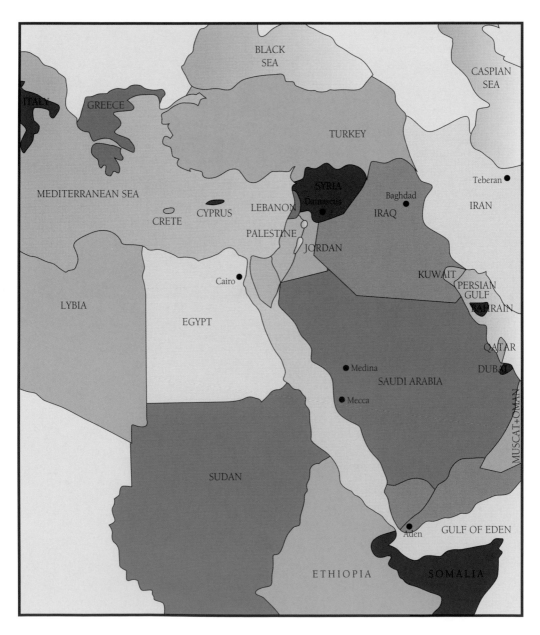

CHAPTER 11

1917-1948 British Mandate

For some readers, the history of the Holy Land is now part of current events rather than history. The aftermath of the First World War brought changes to Europe and the Middle East. New countries were carved out of the now defunct Ottoman Empire: Iraq and Syria, to name but two. Jewish volunteers in the Allied forces served in the Zion Mule Corps in Gallipoli. Others were part of the Jewish Legion, the 38th, 39th and 40th Battalions of the Royal Fusiliers, in which they wore their own insignia.

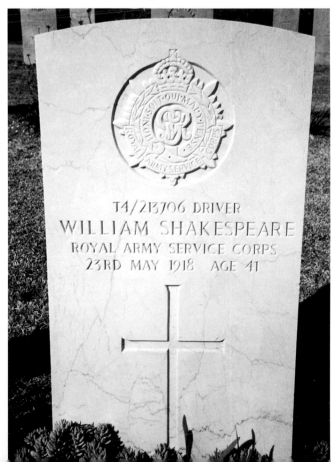

The British army followed almost exactly the route taken by Napoleon in 1799. Napoleon's plan was to take Europe from the rear. This is how the Allies won WWI — Palestine then Bulgaria. Constantinople was menaced, Austria threatened from the rear and that caused their army to lose morale.

The capture of the wells of Be'er Sheva from the Turkish and German armies succeeded, thanks to the courage and perseverance of the ANZACs and the Gurkhas, and opened the way northwards.

Grave in the British military cemetery in Be'er Sheva

The surrender of Jerusalem was a comedy of errors. The Turkish mayor first surrendered to a British mess sergeant and later to the divisional commander. Finally, as befitted the honor of Jerusalem, a formal ceremony was conducted by General Allenby on the steps of the Citadel, just inside the Jaffa Gate.

For the first time since the Crusaders, the Christian holy places were once again under the control of a Christian power. The League of Nations charged the Mandate with enforcing the 1852 Status Quo in the Holy Places, but also recommended that a special committee be formed to determine the rights and claims related to the holy places. To date no such committee has been formed as there is no agreement as to its composition.

YMCA building in Jerusalem

"The present position therefore is that the arrangements existing in 1852 which corresponded to the Status Quo of 1757 as to the rights and privileges of the Christian communities officiating in the Holy Places have to be meticulously observed, and what each rite practised at that time in the way of public worship, decorations of altars and shrines, use of lamps, candelabra, tapestry and pictures, and in the exercise of the most minute acts of ownership and usage has to remain unaltered.... Thus, the Franciscans alone of the Roman Catholic Orders are allowed to celebrate Mass independently in the Holy Places, although the clergy of any Roman Catholic Order can attend. The Patriarch himself, of course, has the right to pontificate. Similarly, of the autocephalous Orthodox Churches, none other than the Orthodox Patriarchate of Jerusalem has any standing in the Holy Places. The Russian Church during the last quarter of the 19th century made strenuous efforts to obtain independent privileges and to maintain altars of their own, for the saying of the Liturgy in the Russian language, but this was successfully opposed by the Hellenic elements. Russian clergy are, however, able to take part in the services. Roman Catholicism now claims the return to the arrangement of 1740, which was in effect the position of the 14th century at the close of the Crusading era, when the majority of the shrines were in the hands of the Latins. This the Orthodox world opposes on the grounds that there is no justice in selecting the rare periods when, as the result of outside political influences, the Latins were for the moment predominant."

L.G.A. Cust, Jerusalem District Officer, July 1929. *The Status Quo in the Holy Places* (Jerusalem: Ariel, 1980)

The restored courtyard of Tel Hai and the monument dedicated to those who fell defending the settlement

The status of France as protector of the Catholic properties terminated. The Catholic Church demanded the return of the Status Quo of 1740 when most of the holy places were under Catholic control. The Orthodox Church, under the Greek Patriarchate of Jerusalem, refused. The Russian Orthodox Church was unsuccessful in obtaining any separate areas or altars within any of the holy sites.

Possibly the most complicated of the holy places is the Church of the Holy Sepulcher, also known as the Church of the Resurrection. The key to the church is held by a Muslim family who open the doors in the morning and close them in the evening. One representative each from the Orthodox, Catholic and Armenian churches are permitted to remain in the Church overnight. In addition to these three churches, the Copts (Egyptian Christians), Syrian Jacobites (Chaldeans) and Abyssinians (Ethiopeans) all have a small part of the church.

In 1929 exact details of the status quo were put in writing and included a clause stating that the authority to repair implies exclusive possession. Repairs to the dome and the roof remained problematical as their ownership was not defined in the original status quo.

In 1920, the League of Nations confirmed the French Mandate over Syria and the British Mandate over Mesopotamia as well as the British undertaking to cre-

Remains of the hydraulic power station, using the waters of the Jordan and Yarmuk rivers, which was destroyed by the invading Iraqi forces in 1948

ate a national home for the Jews in Palestine. The British appointed Feisal king of the newly created Iraq. Land that had belonged to the Turkish Sultan now became British crown land.

Unrest in the French-controlled area of Syria when the Hashemite Emir Feisal was removed from the throne resulted in the attack on Tel Hai and the death of eight defenders, including Joseph Trumpeldor. The resolution of the Jewish settlers to return to Metulla and Tel Hai meant that the Galilee panhandle remained part of Palestine and not part of what would eventually be Lebanon.

In 1923, Palestine was divided. The eastern bank of the Jordan was given to Feisal's brother, the Emir Abdullah, who was made king of the newly created Emirate of Transjordan. With the assistance of British officers, the Jordanian army, known as the Arab Legion, was established

In 1925 their older brother King Ali lost the throne of the Kingdom of the Hejaz and the Hashemite rule of Mecca and Medinah came to an end. The Kingdom of Saudia Arabia was created by Abdul Aziz ibn Saud, its first king, thereby beginning the feud between the Saudi and Hashemite dynasties. (In 1946 the Emirate of Transjordan won complete independence and became the Hashemite Kingdom of Jordan.)

The Jewish national home in Palestine was now limited to the western bank of the Jordan River.

Furthermore, within this area, limitations were placed on the Jews. They could only purchase land along the coastal strip and in the valleys, where the Turks, judging the land to be worthless, had permitted Jewish purchases.

Under the terms of the Mandate the Jewish Agency was recognized as the local autonomous body responsible for the economic and social needs of the Palestinian Jews. This covered schools, hospitals, settlements and the control of the Jewish National Fund, which purchased land using money collected from Jews throughout the world.

Many Arabs from the neighboring areas of Syria and Egypt, and even further afield, continued to come to Palestine, as they had in the Ottoman period, to look for work. Despite setbacks, this was the fastest developing area in the Middle East.

The Palestinian Arabs had the same rights as the Palestinian Jews but were not as well organized. The Muslim community was governed by the Supreme Muslim Council, of whom the mufti was president until he was deposed by the British. The Arab Executive policy was one of non-cooperation.

The 1920s was a decade of economic stagnation — roads were built and forests planted to provide dole work. A Jewish defense organisation, known as the Hagana (defense), grew out of the HaShomer (watchman) organization of the Ottoman period. Mandatory law banned Jews from possessing any weapons, but there was no parallel ban on the Arab population.

The Hagana was unable to offer adequate protection during the widespread Arab riots of 1929 when many Jews were massacred. The surviving Jewish population of Hebron was evacuated by the British.

The Passfield White Paper of 1930 decided that there were to be no further land purchases by Jews and no more Jewish immigration. The reason given for this decision was that a survey had concluded that Palestine was already over-populated and could absorb no more immigrants! World pressure caused these decrees to be abrogated.

Paradoxically, Arab immigration was not curtailed and in fact increased, as demonstrated by journalist Joan Peters in her book *From Time Immemorial*. In the 1931 census the Muslim population is recorded as coming from Syria, Transjordan, Egypt, Hejaz (Arabia), Iraq, Yemen, Algeria, Morocco, Tripoli and Tunis, among other countries.

The general Arab uprising of 1936, organized by the Arab Higher Committee, caused the closure of the port of Jaffa. This resulted in the building of a new port in the fast-growing Jewish town of Tel Aviv. To combat Arab sabotage on the oil pipeline from Iraq to Haifa, Colonel Orde Wingate was sent to organize Jewish volunteers who would operate under the British army.

Members of these field units would be the forerunners of the Israeli Defense Forces, who will always remember the British colonel who led them with a Bible in his hand, exhorting them to take an example from the biblical Israelites, Gideon in particular, and their battles against the numerically superior Canaanites.

During this period over fifty settlements were established on Jewish-owned land in areas where settlement was forbidden. Under Turkish law, the Sultan owned all the land unless he, or his representative, agreed to sell a parcel, which was duly registered (in the "tabu" land registry).

The British Mandate preserved Ottoman law and the sultan's land now became Crown land, which the "crown" could sell if it so desired. The British also preserved the custom that once land had been ploughed the farmer could not be evicted as long as he continued farming, although this did not constitute ownership.

Members of Kibbutz Nahal Oz, a pioneering settlement in the northern Negev, 1951

Holocaust survivors disembark at Haifa

Jewish settlers took advantage of this and overnight a stockade and tower were built and by the time they were detected by the British the land was already ploughed.

In 1939, the first Jew was hanged by the British in the jail in Acco — for being in possession of a pistol.

The rise of the Nazis to power in Germany brought an influx of capital as, on the one hand, the Germans encouraged Jews to leave if they could afford the ransom, and, on the other, the British allowed a limited number of refugees to purchase immigration certificates.

With the outbreak of World War II, Palestinian Jews volunteered for service in the British army but were refused the right to have their own identifying insignia until 1944. Not only were the gates of Palestine closed, but those few vessels reaching the shores with their cargo of refugees were returned to Europe.

Resentment against this policy was kept low-key — the main aim was to defeat the Germans. When it was discovered that the Templars in the German colonies were spying on behalf of the Axis powers, the British rounded them up and shipped them to Australia.

Despite expectations that the end of the war and a change in the British government would alleviate the situation of Holocaust survivors in Europe, this was not to be the case.

UN RESOLUTION & PALESTINE
PARTITION PLAN NOVEMBER 29, 1947

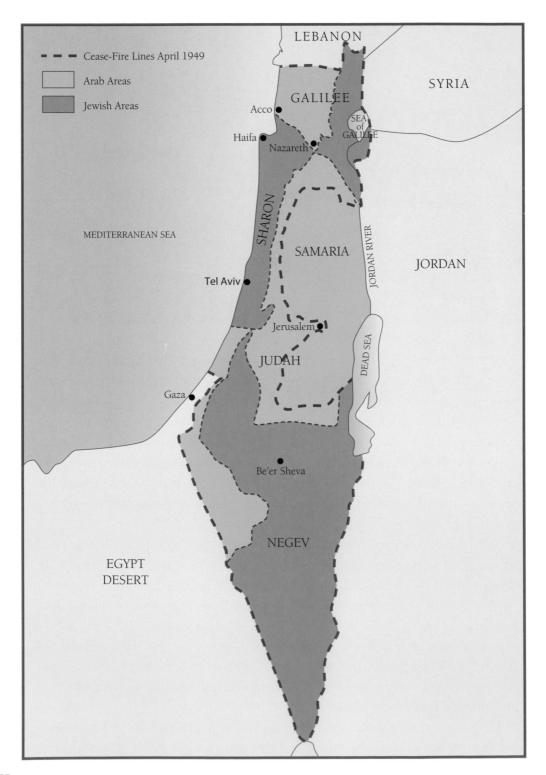

The Haganah and splinter groups the Irgun (Irgun Zvai Leumi, also known as Etzel) and Lehi (Fighters for the Freedom of Israel, called the Stern Gang by the British) all worked towards breaking the British blockade. Some "illegals" safely reached Palestine, others landed but were caught and interned in camps. The more unfortunate were loaded onto British naval ships and taken to Cyprus. The ship *Exodus* was returned to Hamburg.

Members of the Irgun and Lehi began to take more active measures against the British forces such as attacks on army bases, trains, police stations and even the CID headquarters in the King David Hotel in Jerusalem.

Reprisals were severe and included curfews and collective punishment against large and innocent sectors of the general public. The frequent use of the gallows came to an end when two British sergeants held, in vain, as hostages to forestall three death sentences from being carried out were hanged.

"This downward course, which culminated in the relinquishment of the Mandate, could be simply traced by reference, among other things, to each new atrocity in the programme of the Jewish dissident groups" (Major R. Dare Wilson, *Cordon and Search: With 6th Airborne Division in Palestine* [Aldershot, UK: Gale and Polden, 1949], 63).

The British relinquished the Mandate and placed the problem of Palestine in the lap of the United Nations. A committee made up of representatives from eleven neutral countries was sent to Palestine to investigate and suggest a solution.

Under the chairmanship of Jorge Garcia Granados of Guatemala, the solution offered by the UN Special Committee on Palestine was to divide Palestine demographically. Where the population was predominantly Arab that area would be allocated to the Arabs. Where it was predominantly Jewish, it would be allocated to the Jews. The Negev, the southern desert area, was allocated to the Jews because the only patches of green, the only cultivation, was that of the Jewish settlements. Jerusalem, with a population of 100,000 Jews and 20,000 Arabs, was to be declared international. This would be known as "the 1947 UN Partition Plan."

When the UN General Assembly voted on the resolution on November 29, 1947, thirty-three countries voted in favor, including the USA, USSR, and the Commonwealth countries; thirteen voted against, eleven of them Muslim countries; ten abstained, among them Britain. The Arab world was not prepared to consider Jewish independence in any area of Palestine.

Evacuation of the 100,000 British troops began almost immediately. Parallel to the evacuation was the increase of Arab attacks on Jewish transport throughout the country. In many instances, settlements and even towns were under siege. Convoys were ambushed and then massacred and looted by Arab mobs from neighboring villages. The War of Independence had begun.

The realization that the Jewish population could not rely on British protection was brought home when seventy-eight personnel of the Hadassah Hospital on Mount Scopus were massacred in full view of British soldiers.

The Jewish population of Jerusalem, 100,000 in number, were under siege. The water supply to the Jewish section was cut and the supplies of severely rationed food and water were down to a week when the first convoys from the coast reached Jerusalem just in time for the Passover festival. But free and safe access to Jerusalem was not yet to be.

With the departure of the last British forces only days away, David Ben-Gurion, chairman of the National Council, convened a meeting. On the agenda was the recommendation by US Secretary of State Marshall not to establish a state.

"Here you are surrounded by Arabs," he had told the Jewish Agency representative in the US, indicating the Negev. "Here you are surrounded by other Arabs," he continued, pointing to Galilee. "You have Arab states all around you, and your backs are to the sea.... The Arabs have regular well-trained armies and heavy arms. How can you hope to hold out?" (Larry Collins and Dominique Lapierre, O *Jerusalem!* [London: Weidenfeld and Nicolson, 1972], 316).

"I dare believe in victory. We shall triumph!" Ben-Gurion exhorted the council members, the majority of whom voted in favor of proclaiming "the birth of a new Jewish nation in the land of Israel."

The High Commissioner was to lower the Union Jack on Friday at midnight. In order not to desecrate the Sabbath, the Declaration of Independence was made at four o'clock in the afternoon.

On the fifth day of the month of Iyar, in the year 5708 of the Hebrew calendar, May 14, 1948, the State of Israel was born.

> "These Arabs were a new kind of refugee. They fled from Jewish-controlled Palestine as the result of mass panic when the wealthy Arabs, almost to a man, began running away in November 1947, after the UN voted partition. The flight was provoked by lurid tales of Jewish sadism issued by the Mufti and his followers, who presumably intended to whip the Arab population up to resisting the Jews. But the strategy backfired: the warnings and desertion of the Arab elite, together with the only Jewish-executed massacre of the war (the Irgun raid on Deir Yassin on April 9, 1948, in which [an unknown number of Arab men, women and children were killed]), were sufficient to set off the flight.... The Arab masses succumbed to the panic and fled."
>
> James G. McDonald, *My Mission in Israel, 1948-1951* (London: Victor Gollancz, 1951), 160

The Declaration of Independence

In the Land of Israel the Jewish people came into being. In this Land was shaped their spiritul, religious and national character.... Here they...gave to the world the eternal Book of Books....

In 1897 the First Zionist Congress met at the call of Theodore Herzl...and gave public voice to the right of the Jewish people to national restoration in their Land.

This right was acknowledged in the Balfour Declaration on November 2, 1917, and confirmed in the Mandate of the League of Nations, which accorded international validity to the historical connection between the Jewish people and the Land of Israel....

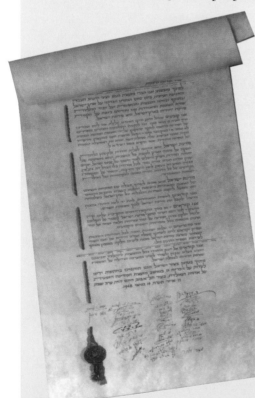

On November 29, 1947, the General Assembly of the United Nations adopted a resolution calling for the establishment of a Jewish state in the Land of Israel...

Accordingly we...proclaim the establishment of...the State of Israel....

It will guarantee freedom of religion and conscience, of language, education and culture. It will safeguard the holy places of all religions. It will be loyal to the principles of the United Nations Charter....

CHAPTER 12

1948- State of Israel

The new state, with no natural resources, without a monetary or postal system, as these had been withdrawn by the British, had barely drawn its first breath when it was bombed by the invading Egyptian army. The armies of Syria, Lebanon, Jordan, Iraq and Saudi Arabia weren't far behind. Other Muslim countries sent additional volunteers and at the same time expelled their Jewish citizens.

With the Soviet Union and the USA in the lead, various nations recognized the new state. Most were sure that the state and its 650,000 Jewish citizens would not survive.

When reviewing the sixty-plus years of Israeli statehood, it appears to be one war after another: the War of Independence (1948-49); the Sinai Campaign (1956); the Six-Day War (1967); the War of Attrition (1967-70); the Yom Kippur War (1973-74); Operation Peace for Galilee (Lebanon 1982); the Second Lebanon War (summer 2006).

Above: David Ben-Gurion reading the Declaration of the Establishment of the State of Israel, Tel Aviv Museum, May 14, 1949
Opposite page: The flag of the State of Israel

Indeed, Israeli war casualties total over eighteen thousand, over six thousand (1 percent of the 1948 population) in the War of Independence alone.

However, between 1948 and 2009, the country absorbed over three million immigrants. In the first two years, almost one and a half million refugees arrived, all of them penniless, most of them without any formal education. Some were remnants of the Holocaust, others had been expelled from Muslim countries. They came from "among the nations, whither they be gone" (Ezekiel 37:21). Yet others came from the free world. The total population of Israel in April 2008 was seven and a half million.

The *ma'abarot* (transit camps), where the immigrants arriving between 1948 and 1951 were housed in tents, are now towns: Beit Shemesh, Or Akiva, Migdal HaEmek, Kiryat Shmona, Kiryat Malachi, Eilat, Yeruham, Shlomi and Sderot. In addition, over two hundred agricultural settlements were established.

These Jewish refugees were never defined as such by the UN High Commission for Refugees, which never assisted in their absorption in Israel. At the time of writing, no compensation for property and assets from any of the Arab countries from which Jews were expelled has been forthcoming.

By the time the next large wave of immigrants arrived in 1955 and 1956, absorption was mainly in new development towns in the underpopulated south. Kiryat Gat, Ofakim, Dimona, Mitzpeh Ramon and Netivot were all founded at that time.

The most recent waves have been from the former USSR (one million) and from Ethiopia. The transfer of nine thousand Ethiopian Jews, in 1990, using all the planes of El Al, the national airline of Israel, and assisted by the Israeli air force, was seen by television viewers throughout the world.

Mekorot, the Israeli water company, completed the national water carrier in 1964 bringing water from Lake Kinneret to the south, thereby fulfilling the biblical prophecy and making the desert bloom once again.

The JNF (Jewish National Fund), which was founded in 1897, has planted over 220 million trees in forests throughout the country. They have developed methods of collecting the maximum amount of rain water and built reservoirs which have brought water sports and recreational fishing to the desert.

New methods of irrigation and farming have been passed on to many Third World countries, some of whom do not, or did not, even recognize the existence of Israel. Medical and technological innovations developed in Israel have become household words all over the world. Indeed, Israel's achievements are many and varied, but it is the wars which interest historians, so let us look at those wars.

The War of Independence

The first stage of the War of Independence lasted from May 15 to June 11, 1948. During that time there were a number of accomplishments:

In the south, even though Yad Mordecai fell, the Egyptian advance towards Tel Aviv was halted. In the center, the Iraqi advance towards Netanya was repulsed. On the Syrian front, Ein Gev fought off an attack but Mishmar HaYarden fell, giving the Syrians a foothold on the western side of the Jordan. In the north, the invasion by Lebanese forces had been prevented but units of the Arab Liberation Army succeeded in penetrating Galilee.

The most crucial battles, though, were probably being fought in the Jerusalem area. The Etzion block, protecting the southern approach to Jerusalem, had fallen and the survivors had been taken prisoner. All attempts to reach the Jewish Quarter in the Old City had failed. Over fifty synagogues and most of the quarter would be destroyed by the Jordanians.

Latrun, which controlled the approach to Jerusalem from the coast, was still held by the Arab Legion. The city was down to two days' ration of bread and even water was severely rationed. Fortunately, a rough dirt track had been discovered quite by chance. Nicknamed the "Burma Road," it was at this point passable to human porters only, but soon would be made fit for donkeys and finally vehicles.

The first truce, supervised by the UN, lasted from June 11 to July 9. During this time, both sides tried to improve their positions. The only agreement secured was the demilitarization of Mount Scopus, where the Hadassah Hospital and Hebrew University were.

During the next ten days of fighting, the Israelis had a number of successes. Part of the Arab population of Lydda and Ramla were expelled when these towns were captured by the Israelis, who had suffered heavy losses. Some fled, but many remained and became Israeli citizens. The Syrians were not dislodged from their bridgehead, but failed to overrun Kibbutz Ayelet HaShahar.

Nazareth surrendered and, after it, all the Arab positions in Lower Galilee including Safed, Tiberias and Beit Shean. As PA President Mahmoud Abbas revealed on al-Palestina TV on July 6, 2009: Fearing retribution for the 1929 massacre of the Jews of Safed, Hebron and Jerusalem, the Arab population of Safed was "motivated to run away.... This was in the memory of our families and our parents.... They realized the balance of forces was shifting; therefore the whole town was abandoned on the basis of this rationale."

Not all the Arabs fled and here too those who remained continued to live in the Galilee and became citizens of Israel. Latrun was still in Jordanian hands but the "Burma Road" was in full use and the railway line connecting Jerusalem to the coast was firmly in Israeli hands, ensuring free access to Jerusalem.

The second truce began on July 18 but was breached almost immediately. The vital springs at Rosh HaAyin were captured and, although the Latrun pumping station, under UN control, was destroyed by the Arab Legion, a hastily laid pipeline along the "Burma Road" restored the water supply to Jerusalem.

Above: Latrun, which symbolized the battle for the road to Jerusalem, no-man's-land until 1967, is now a memorial to the fallen of the Armored Corps
Left: The remains of a truck, part of the many convoys trying to reach besieged Jerusalem

The terms of the truce, rejected by both sides, included making "free ports" of Haifa and Lydda Airport (both held by Israel) and granting Jerusalem and the Negev to the Arabs.

A major effort was now made by the Israeli forces to open the road to the Negev and to clear it of Egyptian troops. The next step was the capture of Be'er Sheva and from there, southwards to Umm Rash Rash (modern Eilat), thereby ensuring Israel's access to the Red Sea.

Some Arabs fled as the Israeli army advanced. As a contemporary news account related, others "panicked and fled ignominiously. Villages were frequently abandoned before they were threatened by the progress of the war" (John Bagot Glubb, London *Daily Mail*, August 12, 1948).

When hostilities ended, many chose not to live under Israeli rule and refused the opportunity to return. Their property was registered by the Custodian of Abandoned Property.

The UN High Commission for Refugees defines a refugee as "one who owing to a well-founded fear of being persecuted…is outside the country of his nationality." The UNHCR has helped well over fifty million refugees, from Europe, Asia and Africa, to resettle or return home. Their children were all absorbed and ceased to be classified as refugees. (Jewish refugees, whether the survivors of the Holocaust or the close to one million expelled from Arab countries with only the clothes on their backs, were all absorbed in Israel without any assistance from the UNHCR.)

A separate UN organization deals only with Palestinian refugees who are defined as "anyone living in Palestine between June 1946 and May 1948." UNRWA, the UN Relief and Works Agency, also extends this refugee status to the children and grandchildren of even one parent or grandparent who qualified, even if the family has been absorbed in its new place of residence.

This is contrary to UN Resolution 194 of November 1948, which resolves "that those refugees wishing to return to their homes and live at peace with their neighbours should be permitted to do so…and compensation should be paid for the property of those choosing not to return." This resolution in no way calls for the right of return for all Palestinian refugees and their descendants.

Those Arabs who remained in the State of Israel make up almost 20 percent of the population of Israel today. As citizens of Israel, they vote in Israeli elections and are represented in the Knesset, Israel's Parliament. Although exempt from service in the Israel Defense Forces, some — mainly Bedouin — do volunteer. With very few exceptions they also do not participate in the National Service programs.

Armistice agreements were signed with Egypt on February 24, 1949, with Jordan on March 4, with Lebanon on March 23, and finally, with Syria on July 20, 1949. These agreements were meant "to facilitate the transition from truce to permanent peace." In actuality, until 1967, the demarcation lines became the de facto borders, despite violations.

The Jewish Palestinians, who had accepted the UN Partition Plan and had survived an Arab-initiated war on all fronts, now had their own state. The Arab

The graves of David Ben-Gurion (shown at right), first prime minister of Israel, and his wife Paula, at Sdeh Boker

"The Secretary General of the Arab League, Azzam Pasha, assured the Arab peoples that the occupation of Palestine would be as simple as a military parade.... All the millions the Jews had spent on land and economic development would be easy booty, for it would be a simple matter to throw the Jews into the Mediterranean.... Brotherly advice was given to the Arabs of Palestine to leave their land and property and stay temporarily in their neighboring fraternal states lest the guns of the invading Arab armies mow them down."

Habib Issa, the New York Lebanese daily Al-Hoda, June 8, 1951

Palestinians, and the Arab world including the Arab League, rejected the same plan, did not succeed in the war they initiated and then did not take advantage of the opportunity history had presented.

In retrospect, while they refer to the creation of the State of Israel as the nakba (tragedy), perhaps the real tragedy for the descendants of those Arab Palestinians is their failure to declare an Arab Palestinian state alongside the Jewish Palestinian state — the State of Israel.

The Gaza Strip now came under Egyptian military occupation. In 1949 the Hashemite Kingdom of Transjordan changed its name to the Hashemite Kingdom of Jordan after annexing those parts of Palestine not included in the State of Israel, generally known as the West Bank. The Arab world opposed this annexation and when the UN voted on it the only country to fully support the move was Pakistan (which actually hoped to annex Kashmir in the same way). The UK partially supported the annexation but rejected its application to east Jerusalem.

Palestine ceased to exist. The Arab population of the West Bank were now Jordanian citizens. Those in the Gaza Strip were denied all elementary rights by the Egyptian military government. At no time in the following eighteen years was there any attempt to create a Palestinian state in the West Bank of Jordan or the Gaza Strip.

During the ensuing eight years there were at least six thousand infiltrations into Israel; over four hundred Israelis were killed and nine hundred injured. Contrary to the terms of the agreements, the UN was not able to assure Israel's access to Jerusalem via Latrun or to the university and hospital on Mount Scopus.

In 1955, Egypt and Syria, who had signed a military pact, began receiving massive arms supplies from the Soviet bloc. Although the US, Britain and France continued to equip the Arab armies, Israel had succeeded in persuading France alone to sell her arms.

Syria attacked Israeli fishing boats on the Kinneret. Terrorist infiltrations from Jordan and Egypt made life in the southern parts of Israel perilous. The Red Sea was closed to Israeli shipping to Eilat. (The Suez Canal had never been open to Israeli vessels.)

Israeli fears of a joint Arab attack coincided with British and French apprehension over the threat posed by Egyptian control over the newly nationalized Suez Canal. The Anglo-French plan to invade Egypt included an Israeli invasion of the Sinai Peninsula.

Sinai Campaign

Between October 29 and November 5, 1956, in what would be known as the Sinai Campaign, Israel conquered the Gaza Strip and the entire Sinai Peninsula, stopping ten miles from the canal. Egypt's military infrastructure in Sinai was severely damaged, the Gulf of Eilat was reopened and the terrorist bases were destroyed.

Due to heavy US pressure, the Anglo-French invasion of Egypt accomplished nothing. US threats to expel Israel from the UN and to impose economic sanctions, together with a guarantee by the UN and all the major maritime powers assuring freedom of navigation for Israel — both in the canal and in the gulf — and UN control of the Gaza Strip (a base for terrorist attacks on Israel), secured a complete Israeli withdrawal from Sinai.

In no time at all the guarantees were shown to be worthless. The canal was never opened to Israeli shipping and the Egyptians replaced the UN administration of the Gaza Strip.

Egypt and Syria united to form the United Arab Republic, and their attempts to "lead" the Arab world resulted in US intervention in the civil war in Lebanon and Anglo-US support to keep secure Jordan's throne for King Hussein, with the agreement of Israel, who permitted use of her airspace.

After a few years of relative quiet, terrorist infiltrations were once more on the increase, penetrating to the heart of the country. Syrian positions bombarded Israel's northern settlements. President Nasser of Egypt unilaterally ordered UN troops to leave Sinai, where they had been stationed since 1957, and moved his army in.

Once more the Straits of Tiran were closed to Israeli shipping. Pacts were signed between Egypt and Jordan, Iraq, Kuwait and Algeria, and the Arab world prepared for war against Israel. "In five days we shall liquidate the State of Israel" was the official forecast of the Egyptian army. "Four days," was the Syrian prophecy.

According to international law, war had been declared on Israel. Anticipating her impending destruction, the impotent world looked on. Only France acted — by decreeing an arms embargo on Israel.

The Six-Day War

It was clear that Israel had only herself to rely on and so, on June 5, 1967, a preemptive air strike was launched. Within hours, over four hundred Egyptian planes were destroyed. Within four days the Israeli forces had taken the entire

Paratroopers at the Western Wall, Six-Day War, 1967

Sinai Peninsula and were on the banks of the Suez Canal.

Explaining why he agreed to a cease-fire, Nasser said: "We had no defenses on the west side of the canal. Not a single soldier stood between the enemy and the capital."

Intermediaries, including UN mediator General Odd Bull, advised King Hussein that Israel had no intention of attacking Jordan. Jordan however chose to ignore Israeli assurances and joined the war, opening fire along the entire border, shelling even the coastal towns of Netanya, Herzliya and Tel Aviv. The main brunt of the attack was, of course, Jerusalem.

Within three days, the Israeli army was on the banks of the Jordan River. The capture of the Old City of Jerusalem resulted in heavy Israeli casualties because of the desire not to inflict any damage on the holy sites. Jews had free access to the Temple Mount — for the first time since the Romans destroyed the Temple in the year 70 CE.

Due to the strategic and topographic advantage of the Syrian positions and the ineffectiveness of Israeli bombing, the Israeli forces had not advanced in the north. When Syria rejected the cease-fire agreed upon by Egypt and Jordan, the decision was made to advance, despite the knowledge that the Israeli losses would be high. Within thirty hours the Israeli army had taken the entire Golan Heights and was on the main road leading to Damascus.

The Israelis were euphoric. Surely Jordan, and possibly Egypt, would join Israel

ISRAEL, JUNE 1967

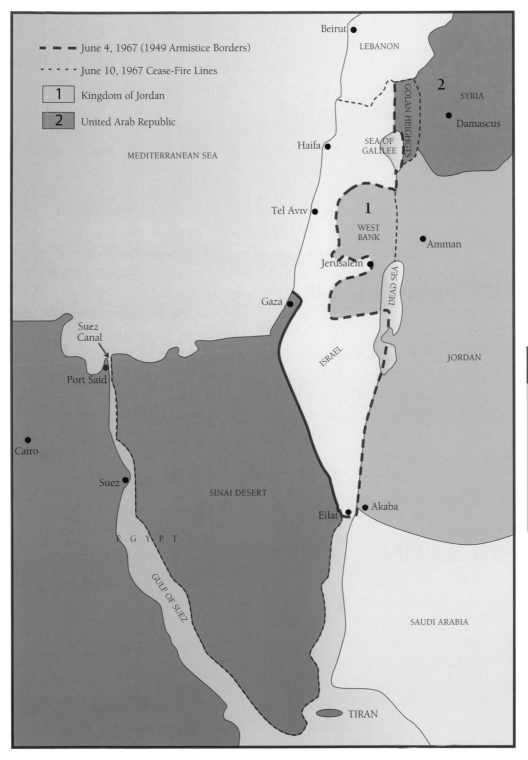

- — — June 4, 1967 (1949 Armistice Borders)
- - - - June 10, 1967 Cease-Fire Lines
- **1** Kingdom of Jordan
- **2** United Arab Republic

Beirut
LEBANON

2 SYRIA

Damascus

GOLAN HEIGHTS

MEDITERRANEAN SEA

Haifa

SEA OF GALILEE

Tel Aviv

1
WEST
BANK

Amman

Jerusalem

DEAD SEA

Gaza

ISRAEL

JORDAN

Suez
Canal

Port Said

Cairo

Suez

SINAI DESERT

Akaba

Eilat

E G Y P T

GULF OF SUEZ

SAUDI ARABIA

TIRAN

in direct face-to-face talks which would lead to full-fledged peace treaties combined with an Israeli withdrawal.

The careful wording of UN Security Council Resolution 242 (November 22, 1967) deliberately did not call for the withdrawal from all territories acquired by Israel as a result of the war. It did however call for a termination of belligerency and the right of every state in the area to live in peace within secure and recognized boundaries.

The Palestinians are not mentioned in the resolution (with the exception of the refugees), as up to that point there had never been a demand to establish a separate Palestinian entity although the Palestine Liberation Organization had been formed in 1964, primarily to conduct operations against the State of Israel. Similarly the resolution made no attempt to call for the establishment of a Palestinian state in the areas of the West Bank, which had been annexed by the Hashemite Kingdom of Jordan, or the Gaza Strip, in which the rule was by Egyptian military government.

Reality was different. At the Arab summit in Khartoum in September 1967, paragraph 3 of the resolutions, which were passed unanimously, states, "This will be done within the framework of the main principles by which the Arab States abide, namely, no peace with Israel, no recognition of Israel, no negotiations with it."

Israeli agricultural settlements in the Jordan and Beit Shean Valleys were shelled from Jordan and terrorist infiltrations posed a constant threat and a cycle of reprisals continued. Through it all the bridges connecting the West Bank — and indirectly Israel — with Jordan, and ultimately the Arab world, remained open. Terrorists resorted to new tactics: the hijacking of an El Al airplane to Algeria.

War of Attrition

Based on the assumption that, because the Israeli army consisted mainly of reservists, the economy would not be able to withstand long-term mobilization, the Egyptians began what would be known as the "War of Attrition." The main aim was to lower morale within Israel by inflicting daily casualties. Israeli retaliation was deep within Egypt and included bringing captured Russian radar equipment back intact.

Russian crews manned newly installed SAM-2 and SAM-3 missiles and flew Soviet aircraft, four of them brought down by Israel Air Force planes. Fearing a confrontation with Russia, US Secretary of State Rogers pressured Israel to set aside her demand for direct negotiations.

UN Ambassador Jarring brokered a cease-fire between Israel and Egypt and Jordan, as a preview to direct talks. Within days, and in direct contravention of the terms of the agreement, Russia installed anti-aircraft missiles along the entire eastern front. The seeds for the 1973 war had been sown.

In September 1970, henceforth to be known as "Black September," King Hussein expelled all the Palestinian terrorist organizations from Jordan. The PLO claimed that over twenty thousand casualties had been inflicted by the Jordanian army.

Syrian forces invaded Jordan but retreated when Israel openly moved military units to the Syrian border and, in conjunction with the US, Israel advised both Syria and Russia that any interference in Jordan would have severe consequences.

The Palestinian terrorist organizations had not yet gained a foothold in Lebanon and most of their early activities were directed against Israeli and Jewish targets throughout the world. Over the next three years the borders were reasonably quiet, but this was merely the lull before the storm.

The Yom Kippur War

The storm broke on October 6, 1973, on the afternoon of Yom Kippur (the Day of Atonement). Deluded by the conviction that Egypt was not ready for another war and that Syria would not go to war without Egypt, Israel was taken completely unawares.

In the south, the Egyptian forces crossed the canal to be faced by about six hundred unprepared reservists, many of them in the middle of praying. Two hundred kilometers (125 miles) separated the canal from Israel.

Within hours the Egyptian forces had prepared ten bridges and fifty ferries and were streaming into Sinai, under an umbrella of Russian missiles against which the Israel Air Force was virtually defenseless. After a week of fighting, their maximum penetration was ten kilometers (6 miles) along the length of the canal.

In the north, waves of Syrian forces swept onto the Golan, twenty-five kilometers (15 miles) east to west at its widest point. They advanced towards the Kinneret, protected by the same Russian umbrella.

In forty-eight hours they reached their maximum penetration — five kilometers from the Bnot Yaacov bridge over the Jordan River. On October 8, the Israeli counterattack began and by the 10th the Israeli forces had reached the former cease-fire lines. Damascus was forty kilometers away.

Israeli appeals to the US, her only supplier for replacements to her depleted armory, were answered by evasion — President Nixon and Secretary of State Kissinger wanted a "limited Israeli defeat." The Russian airlift continued unabated.

Kissinger tried to negotiate a cease-fire in situ by which the Egyptians would be in control of the entire canal. When President Sadat refused, the US decided to begin its airlift. Europe united in its refusal to allow American planes refueling rights, thereby causing an added delay. Eventually the planes were permitted to refuel at the American-leased base in the Azores.

The tide on the Egyptian front began to turn on October 15 when Israeli units crossed the canal westwards. Only on the 21st did Egypt acknowledge this presence, but by then the Egyptian Third Army was under siege and Cairo was threatened. Convinced by Russia and the US that things could only get worse, Egypt agreed to the UN Security Council Resolution 383, which called on the parties to terminate all military activity immediately, in the positions they occupy, and begin implementation of UN Resolution 242 and negotiations "aimed at establishing a just and durable peace in the Middle East."

Sporadic fighting continued as the Egyptian forces tried to improve their positions, to no avail. Israel allowed medical supplies through to the besieged Third Army.

On the 27th, fighting finally ended. Israel lost over 2,500 soldiers. With a population of two and a half million, this was a tenth of a percent of the population (a percentage that would amount to around three million people in the United States today). An agreement with Egypt was signed on January 18, 1974.

On the Syrian front, fighting continued until a similar agreement was signed on May 31, 1974. It was only in 1981 that a law was passed by the Knesset formally annexing the Golan Heights and making them an integral part of the State of Israel. Israeli citizenship was offered to the Druze villagers, none of whom had left in the wars of 1967 or 1973, but for the most part this offer was rejected.

Israeli Settlements

Up until 1974, apart from security settlements in the Jordan Valley (the de facto border between Israel and Jordan after 1967), the only Israeli settlements in the West Bank and Gaza Strip were on property legally owned by Jews prior to the establishment of the State of Israel in 1948.

The Jews of Hebron had been forcibly removed by the British in the 1920s after the Arab pogroms against their Jewish neighbors. In some instances those homes were cared for by Arabs until the owners', or their heirs', return in 1967. The Etzion bloc had been conquered by the Jordanian army immediately before the establishment of Israel in May 1948 and those not massacred had been taken prisoners of war. The survivors returned to what was left of their homes. The same was true of the first settlers in the Gaza Strip who rebuilt the agricultural settlements that had been totally destroyed by the Egyptian invading army in 1948.

Only in 1974, when there was no sign of negotiations with Jordan on the horizon, were the first "West Bank settlements" established.

Egypt

In 1977, very faint winds of change began to blow; President Sadat visited Israel and addressed the Knesset. At Camp David, on March 26, 1979, the first peace between Israel and one of her neighbors was signed by Menachem Begin and

President Anwar Sadat, President Jimmy Carter and Prime Minister Menachem Begin at Camp David signing the Camp David Accords, 1978

Anwar Sadat. Within two years Israel had withdrawn from the entire Sinai Peninsula, and Egypt and Israel established diplomatic relations. President Sadat would later pay with his life for this brave move.

Despite the peace treaty, relations between the two countries remain very cool and Egyptians visiting Israel are often boycotted by their associates.

Hashemite Kingdom of Jordan

Already in 1949 Jordan offered citizenship to all Palestinians who wished to claim it. The Arab League opposed this plan and no other Arab government followed Jordan's lead (according to the Jordanian state publication *Jordan Diary 1998*).

On July 20, 1951, King Abdullah, while at Friday morning prayers with his grandson Hussein, was assassinated. When he turned eighteen in May 1953, Hussein became the third king of the Hashemite Kingdom of Jordan. (His father was not fit to rule.)

In 1964 the Palestine Liberation Organization was formed. The 1960s also saw the rise of independent guerrilla groups (*fedayeen*), including the Fatah. After the loss of the West Bank in 1967, Jordan continued to pay the salaries and pensions of civil servants and to administer the religious properties and educational affairs.

Palestinian *fedayeen* groups, which had gained strength and expected immunity from Jordan's laws, were causing virtual anarchy in Jordan, particularly along the Jordan Valley, from which they crossed into Israel to carry out their

The Israel-Jordan Peace Treaty signing ceremony in the Arava, 1994

terrorist attacks on the Israeli civilian population. They also tried to assassinate King Hussein. On an international level, they were responsible for a wave of airline hijackings.

In September 1970, when Syrian tanks were poised on Jordan's borders in support of the Palestinian terrorist groups, King Hussein took matters into hand. Thousands of members of the terrorist organizations were killed. Those who survived were expelled and transferred their headquarters to south Lebanon.

In response to this act a new Palestinian terrorist organization — Black September — was formed and in 1972 members of this organization massacred eleven Israeli sportsmen at the Olympic Games in Munich.

Free of terrorist disruption, and with Israeli technology and assistance, the villages along the Jordan Valley developed their agriculture and exported their products to the Arab world. On July 31, 1988, King Hussein announced the severance of all administrative and legal ties with the West Bank, excluding the Hashemite guardianship over the holy sites in Jerusalem.

When Iraq invaded Kuwait on August 2, 1990, Jordan did not join the coalition, which included the Western powers and most of the Arab world. During the ensuing war Israel was hit by a number of Scud missiles fired from Iraq but acceded to the coalition request not to retaliate. The Arab population of Israel and the West Bank supported Saddam Hussein during this war and as a result all the Palestinians working in Kuwait, many of whom had been there decades, were expelled. A large number were absorbed in Jordan.

The three-day Madrid Peace Conference at the end of October 1991 was the beginning of a chain of events which has not yet ended.

Immediately thereafter, the first bilateral and direct talks between Israel and

Jordan, Lebanon, Syria and the Palestinians were conducted. Almost two years later the Israeli-Jordanian Common Agenda was signed. The meeting of an Israeli and a Jordanian delegation at Ein Avrona (north of Eilat and Akaba) paved the way for the historic meeting, in Washington on July 25, 1994, between King Hussein and Israeli Prime Minister Yitzhak Rabin.

On October 26, 1994, the Jordan-Israel Peace Treaty was signed, thereby defining the international border between Israel and Jordan and normalizing relations between the two countries. Despite the peace treaty, here too the relationship remains very cool and Jordanians visiting Israel to attend international conferences are often boycotted by their associates.

Lebanon

Since their expulsion from Jordan in 1970 the various Palestinian terrorist groups had successfully taken over southern Lebanon. Almost daily, or nightly, Katyusha rockets were fired into Israeli towns and settlements, from Nahariya in the west to Metulla and Kiryat Shmona in the east. In March 1978 Israel invaded Lebanon up to the Litani River to clear the terrorist bases and then withdrew in compliance with UN Resolution 425, which also established a UN Interim Force for south Lebanon to ensure that attacks on Israel would cease.

They didn't. Katyusha rockets continued to rain on the northern towns of Israel. So, on June 5, 1982, Operation Peace for Galilee began. Israeli troops, welcomed by Lebanese villagers, once again crossed the border. Although Israeli troops advanced as far as Beirut and the Bekaa Valley, expulsion of all the terrorist organizations was only partially achieved; their leadership, however, was exiled to Tunis. An agreement was signed between Israel and Lebanon on May 17, 1983, and once again the Israel Defense Forces withdrew.

This time, however, the withdrawal was not complete and Israel continued to patrol a fourteen-kilometer strip, within Lebanon, along the border with Israel, initially together with the South Lebanese Army. Due to Syrian de facto control over Lebanon's policies and decision-making process, all attempts at negotiations with the government of Lebanon failed.

To counter the continuous attacks on the northern Israeli towns and villages, which were now carried out by the Iranian-backed Hizbullah, Israel launched the "Grapes of Wrath" in April 1996. In a document of understanding initiated by US mediation it was proposed that negotiations be conducted between Israel and Lebanon as well as Israel

The Good Fence, border between Israel and Lebanon

and Syria, which had over thirty thousand Syrian soldiers stationed in Lebanon.

On April 1, 1998, Israel's Ministerial Committee for National Security issued an announcement that called on the Lebanese government to "restore its effective control over Southern Lebanon and assume responsibility for guaranteeing that its territory will not be used a base for terrorist activity against Israel," while announcing its decision to withdraw all Israeli troops from the security belt.

The withdrawal was completed in May 2000 and on June 18, 2000, UN Security Council Resolution 1701 confirmed that Israel had indeed withdrawn its forces from Lebanon in accordance with Security Council Resolution 425.

Hizbullah attacks on Israel did not cease and in July 2006 after the kidnapping of Israeli soldiers and a lethal barrage on Israeli cities including the port city of Haifa, Israel entered into a full-scale war against Hizbullah. The pretext given by Hizbullah was that the Israeli withdrawal from Lebanon was not complete and, as of writing, there is a demand that Israel withdraw from the Shab'a Farms, the village of Ajar.

This small village was part of the Syrian Golan Heights captured by Israel in the course of the Six-Day War in 1967. It was never part of Lebanon and the villagers are Syrian Alawi who are unwilling to become part of Lebanon. Their fate is unfolding as you read these words.

During the Second Lebanon War one-third of Israel's population was within range of Hizbullah missiles. Over one million Israelis, including those in Kiryat Shmona, Nahariya, Acco, Haifa, Carmiel and Tiberias, were forced to live in bomb shelters.

Hizbullah, supported by Syria and Iran, continues to pose a serious threat to Israel's security in the north. UN patrols meant to ensure that Hizbullah is not rearming are ineffectual and long-range rockets from Iran have been placed in homes and mosques in the villages close to the border with Israel. The government of Lebanon and its army are acquiescent.

Syria

The official Syrian position is the return of the entire Golan Heights in return for peace with Israel. Israel, which was forced to capture the Golan Heights twice, each time after being attacked by Syria, each time at great cost, is wary. There do not seem to be bilateral talks at the moment and Syria is still very much under Iranian influence.

Palestinians

Initially the PLO and other terrorist organizations conducted their attacks on Israel from Jordan. After their expulsion by Jordan in 1970 the Palestinian leadership moved to Lebanon, from which they were exiled to Tunis in 1982.

In December 1987 what was to be known as the First Intifada (uprising) erupted, ending with the Madrid Conference in October 1991. This conference ultimately led to the Israel-Jordan Peace Treaty. It also led to the return of the Tunisian exilees to the West Bank and the Gaza Strip and to direct, albeit secret, negotiations between Israel and the Palestinians.

At the conclusion of these lengthy negotiations in Oslo, on September 9, 1993, in a letter to Israeli Prime Minister Rabin, the chairman of the PLO, Yasser Arafat, affirmed that the PLO recognized the right of Israel to exist (although the PLO charter was never formally amended to include this "recognition"). This was considered a major breakthrough as the entire Arab world, excluding Egypt in 1979 and Jordan in 1994, refused (and still refuses as of November 2009) to acknowledge Israel's creation in 1948.

This undertaking to change the PLO covenant, to renounce the use of terrorism and to reach a peaceful resolution of the conflict between Israel and the Palestinians resulted in a meeting between Prime Minister Rabin and Yasser Arafat in Washington on September 13, 1993. Thereafter the joint Israeli-Palestinian Declaration of Principles (DOP) was signed.

Over the next decade the world donated more than $2 billion to the Palestinian Authority to set up an economic infrastructure, very little of that coming from the oil-rich Arab countries. As there was no system of audit and accountability, most of these funds were squandered.

Despite the donations from the UN, the US, the EU, individual European and Scandinavian countries and Japan, there is no modern hospital in the West Bank or the Gaza Strip. There is however a well-equipped terrorist infrastructure including long-range rockets.

A series of agreements followed over the next seven years. The Gaza-Jericho Agreement, signed in Cairo in May 1994, recognized Palestinian self-rule in the Gaza Strip and the Jericho area. Israeli military forces were withdrawn and authority was transferred from the Israeli Civil Administration to the Palestinian Authority. The casino subsequently built in Jericho was visited daily by hundreds of Israelis.

By February 1995 the area of self-rule included all the major cities in the West Bank (Bethlehem, Jenin, Nablus, Kalkilya, Tulkarem and Ramallah, but excluding Hebron). Ninety-five percent of the Palestinian population, including about 450 towns and villages, came under direct Palestinian rule.

Israel continued to maintain control of the West Bank settlements as well as all of the state land (that which had belonged to the Turkish sultan, then the British crown and finally the Jordanian crown).

In January 1996 elections were held for the Palestinian Council and Yasser Arafat was elected head of the Palestinian Authority. Thereafter the council voted to amend those articles in the Palestine National Charter which contradict the DOP of 1993. However the charter was never legally amended and the call for armed struggle in Article 9 was never abrogated.

Despite a joint communiqué at the negotiations on the permanent status arrangements held at Taba in May 1996, there was no progress in the matters of Jerusalem, refugees, settlements and security.

In the Wye River Memorandum signed in October 1998, Israel undertook further withdrawals and the Palestinians pledged to prevent further acts of terrorism, to collect all illegal weapons and to revoke those sections of the Palestinian National Charter which called for the destruction of Israel. When Yasser Arafat failed to act on these commitments and announced his decision to unilaterally declare an independent Palestinian state, negotiations were temporarily halted but then continued at meetings at Sharm el-Sheikh, at the Erez checkpoint and in Washington.

At the July 2000 Camp David Summit both Israel and the Palestinians agreed, according to the trilateral statement released after the summit, "that the aim of their negotiations is to put an end to decades of conflict and achieve a just and lasting peace" and "to conclude an agreement on all permanent status issues as soon as possible."

Prime Minister Ehud Barak's offer, brokered by President Clinton, to transfer 91 percent of the West Bank was rejected by Yasser Arafat, who left the summit without making a counteroffer. Rejected too was an amended offer by President Clinton for 97 percent of the West Bank, all of the Gaza Strip, a capital in Jerusalem and a $30 billion fund to compensate refugees.

According to the Mitchell Report the intifada that erupted in September 2000 was premeditated and not spontaneous. Although the unabated Palestinian violence and continued suicide bombings prevented any further in-depth negotiations, in April 2003 US President George W. Bush presented the "Road Map" solution to the conflict.

The cessation of all terrorist acts promised by the Palestinian terrorist factions in June 2003 lasted less than two months. In response Israel froze the diplomatic process with the PA and initiated targeted attacks on the terrorist leadership.

Following an understanding between US President Bush and Israeli Prime Minister Sharon supporting adjustments to the 1949 lines, and the February 2005 pledge by Palestinian Authority Chairman Mahmoud Abbas to Sharon — in the presence of Egyptian President Hosni Mubarak and King Hussein of Jordan — that if the Israelis desisted from all further attacks against the Palestinians, the Palestinians would stop all acts of violence against Israel, Israel unilaterally decided to evacuate the Gaza Strip.

In August 2006 the Israel Defense Forces withdrew from the entire Gaza Strip and every Israeli settlement was forcibly evacuated. Instead of utilizing the extensive agriculture infrastructure the Israeli settlers had so successfully operated, the Arab residents of Gaza destroyed what remained of the Israeli settlements, including many of the synagogues. The schools were converted into terrorist bases from which rockets could be fired into Israel.

In June 2007 Hamas, a fundamentalist terrorist organization headed by Ismail Haniyeh, forcibly took control of the Gaza Strip, imprisoning and murdering supporters of Mahmoud Abbas belonging to the Fatah Party, the largest faction of the PLO.

The barrage of rockets from the Gaza Strip on towns and villages in the south of Israel increased in frequency, potential destructive power and range reaching the towns of Ashkelon, Ashdod and Yavneh. Paradoxically, the rockets fired by the Palestinians endangered the power station that provided them with most of their electricity.

The Israeli "Operation Cast Lead" in January 2009 brought a respite to a million Israelis living in the south, targeting Hamas weapons storage facilities, missile-launching sites, smuggling tunnels and operatives.

From here on YOU are a witness to the events. I hope that you will follow them with greater interest and understanding, now that you have a deeper knowledge of this tiny, but turbulent, corner of the world.

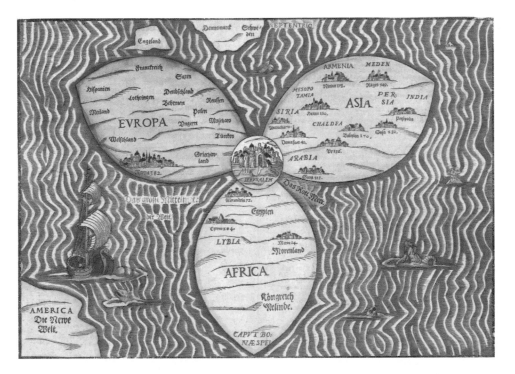

"I will take the children of Israel from among the nations, whither they be gone, and will gather them on every side, and bring them into their own land: and I will make them one nation in the land upon the mountains of Israel…. And the nations shall know that I the Lord do sanctify Israel when My sanctuary shall be in the midst of them for evermore."

Ezekiel 37:21-22, 28

BIBLIOGRAPHY

The bibliography does not list every source used in writing this book. Hebrew references have been omitted as have academic publications. Each book listed has its own bibliography for those really bitten by the history bug.

Use the bibliography as a stepping-stone along the historical path in which you are most interested. Browse in your local library and bookshop. For those whose "appetites" have merely been "whetted," a representative selection of novels has been included.

Ben-Sasson, H. H., ed. *A History of the Jewish People*. London: Weidenfeld and Nicolson, 1976.

Benvenisti, Meron. *The Crusaders in the Holy Land*. New York: Macmillan, 1970.

Canaan, Tewfik. *Mohammedan Saints and Sanctuaries in Palestine*. 1927. Reprint, Jerusalem: Ariel, 1990.

Collins, Larry, and Dominique Lapierre. *O Jerusalem!* London: Weidenfeld and Nicolson, 1972.

Cohen, Abraham, ed. *Soncino Books of the Bible*. 14 vols. Hindhead, Surrey, UK: Soncino Press, 1945–1952.

Comay, Joan. *The World's Greatest Story: The Epic of the Jewish People in Biblical Times*. London: Weidenfeld and Nicolson, 1978.

Cornfield, Gaalyah, and D. N. Freedman. *Archaeology of the Bible: Book by Book*. New York: Harper and Row, 1976.

Cust, L. G. A. *The Status Quo in the Holy Places*. Jerusalem: Ariel, 1980.

Danby, Herbert, trans. *The Mishnah*. London: Oxford University Press, 1933.

Dimont, Max I. *Jews, God and History*. New York: Simon and Schuster, 1962.

Dudman, Helga, and Ruth Kark. *The American Colony: Scenes from a Jerusalem Saga*. Jerusalem: Carta, 1998.

Harkabi, Yehoshafat. *The Palestinian Covenant and Its Meaning*. London: Valentine Mitchell, 1979.

Hitti, Philip. *History of Syria: Including Lebanon and Palestine*. New York: Macmillan, 1951.

Hockstein, Joseph M., and Murray S. Greenfield. *The Jews' Secret Fleet*. Jerusalem: Gefen Publishing House, 1987.

Holmes, Reed M. *The Forerunners: The Tragic Story of 156 Down-East Americans Led to Jaffa in 1866 by Charismatic G. J. Adams to Plant the Seeds of Modern Israel*. Independence, MO: Herald Publishing House, 1981.

Idinopulos, Thomas A. *Jerusalem Blessed, Jerusalem Cursed: Jews, Christians, and Muslims in the Holy City from David's Time to Our Own*. Chicago: Ivan R. Dee, 1991.

Jordan Diary 1998. Amman, Jordan: International Press Office of the Royal Hashemite Court, 1998.

Josephus, Flavius. *The Complete Works of Josephus*. Translated by William Whiston. Grand Rapids, MI: Kregel Publications, 1960.

Kaufman, Yehezkel. *The Religion of Israel from Its Beginnings to the Babylonian Exile*. Translated and abridged by Moshe Greenberg. New York: Schocken, 1972.

Kobler, Franz. *Napoleon and the Jews*. New York: Schocken, 1976.

Kushner, David, ed. *Palestine in the Late Ottoman Period: Political, Social and Economic Transformation*. Jerusalem: Yad Izhak Ben Zvi, 1986.

Le Strange, Guy. *Palestine under the Moslems: A Description of Syria and the Holy Land*. London, 1890. Reprint, New York: AMS Press, 1975.

Lorch, Netanel. *One Long War*. Jerusalem: Keter, 1976.

Maccoby, Hyam, ed. and trans. *Judaism on Trial: Jewish-Christian Disputations in the Middle Ages*. London: The *Littman* Library of Jewish Civilization, 1993.

Martin, Richard C. *Islam: A Cultural Perspective*. Englewood Cliffs, NJ: Prentice Hall, 1982.

Munro, Dana C. "Urban and the Crusaders." In *Translations and Reprints from the Original Sources of European History*, vol. 1:2. Philadelphia: University of Pennsylvania, 1895, 5-8.

The New Testament. Various editions.

Payne, Robert. *The Dream and the Tomb: A History of the Crusades*. New York: Dorset Press, 1984.

Oliphant, Laurence. *Haifa, or Life in Modern Palestine*. Edinburgh and London: William Blackwood and Sons, 1887. Elibron Classics Series. Chestnut Hill, MA: Adamant Media Corporation, 2005.

Peters, Joan. *From Time Immemorial: The Origins of the Arab-Jewish Conflict over Palestine*. London: Michael Joseph, 1985.

Pickthall, Mohammed Marmaduke, trans. *The Meaning of the Glorious Koran*. Albany, NY: SUNY Press, 1976.

Pixner, Bargil. *With Jesus through Galilee According to the Fifth Gospel*. Translated by C. Botha and D. Foster. Rosh Pina, Israel: Corazin, 1992.

Pritchard, J. B., ed. *Ancient Near Eastern Texts Relating to the Old Testament*. Princeton, NJ: Princeton University Press, 1950.

Regan, Geoffrey. *Saladin and the Fall of Jerusalem*. London: Croom Helm, 1987.

Rowley, Harold Henry. *The Growth of the Old Testament*. New York: Harper Torchbooks, 1963.

Schiffman, Lawrence H. *Reclaiming the Dead Sea Scrolls: The History of Judaism, the Background of Christianity, the Lost Library of Qumran*. Philadelphia: Jewish Publication Society, 1994.

Scholem, Gershom. *Kabbalah*. Jerusalem: Keter, 1974

Schroeder, Gerald L. *Genesis and the Big Bang*. New York: Bantam, 1990.

Schur, Nathan. *Twenty Centuries of Christian Pilgrimage to the Holy Land*. Tel Aviv: Dvir, 1992.

Spirydon, S. N., trans. Neophytos, *Extracts from Annals of Palestine, 1821–1841*. Compiled by Eli Schiller. Jerusalem: Ariel, 1979. Originally published in *Journal of the Palestine Oriental Society* 18 (1938).

Steinsaltz, Adin. *The Essential Talmud*. New York: Bantam, 1976.

Stern, Ephraim, ed. *The New Encyclopedia of Archaeological Excavations in the Holy Land*. 4 vols. Jerusalem: Israel Exploration Society and Carta, 1993.

Sykes, Christopher. *Crossroads to Israel: Palestine from Balfour to Bevin*. London: Collins, 1965.

Twain, Mark. *The Innocents Abroad*. Hartford, CT: American Publishing Company, 1869.

VanderKam, James C. *The Dead Sea Scrolls Today*. Grand Rapids, MI: William B. Eerdmans, 1994.

Vester, Bertha Spafford. *Our Jerusalem: An American Family in the Holy City, 1881–1949*. Jerusalem: Ariel, 1988.

Wilson, Major R. Dare. *Cordon and Search: With 6th Airborne Division in Palestine*. Aldershot, UK: Gale and Polden, 1949.

Yadin, Yigael. *Bar Kokhba*. London: Weidenfeld and Nicolson, 1971.

—. *Hazor: The Rediscovery of a Great Citadel of the Bible*. London: Weidenfeld and Nicolson, 1975.

—. *Masada: Herod's Fortress and the Zealots' Last Stand*. London: Weidenfeld and Nicolson, 1966.

—. *The Temple Scroll: The Hidden Law of the Dead Sea Sect*. London: Weidenfeld and Nicolson, 1985.

Journals

Biblical Archaeologist. American Schools of Oriental Research.

Biblical Archaeology Review. Biblical Archaeology Society.

Novels

Auel, Jean M. *The Clan of the Cave Bear*. New York: Crown, 1980.

Michener, James. *The Source*. New York: Random House, 1965.

Steinberg, Milton. *As a Driven Leaf*. New York: Behrman House, 1939.

Uris, Leon. *Exodus*. New York: Doubleday, 1958.

M. *The Haj*. Franklin Center, PA: Franklin Library, 1984.

Wouk, Herman. *The Hope*. Boston: Little, Brown, 1993.

GENERAL INDEX
The index includes people, places and subjects.

* places appearing on the general map on page 9 followed by their reference number on that map
\# places appearing on other maps or in photographs followed by the relevant page number
ff forward from the page mentioned

List of Maps